Church Planting
for Reproduction

Church Planting for Reproduction

Samuel D. Faircloth

Foreword by Arthur P. Johnston

BAKER BOOK HOUSE
Grand Rapids, Michigan 49516

Copyright 1991 by
Baker Book House Company

Library of Congress Cataloging-in-Publication Data

Faircloth, Samuel D.
      Church planting for reproduction / Samuel D. Faircloth; foreword
by Arthur P. Johnston.
                    p.   cm.
      Includes bibliographical references and index.
      ISBN 0-8010-3558-9
      1. Church development, New. 2. Church growth. I. Title.
BV652.24.F35 1991
254'.1—dc20
                                                                                    90-44359
                                                                                        CIP

To my sacrificial and loving wife,

Arliss,

and our daughters,

Rebecca, Martha, Priscilla,

Ruth, Elizabeth, Anne, and Miriam:

deeply involved partners in ministry.

Contents

Part 1: Introduction

Part 2: The Preparatory and Pioneer Periods

Part 3: The Period of Growth and Organization

Part 4: The Period of Reproduction

List of Figures

Chapter 6

Chapter 7

Chapter 8

Chapter 9

Chapter 10

Chapter 11

Chapter 12

Foreword

Church planting has been at the heart of the Great Commission of missionary and church ministry from the time of the Apostles to today. Jesus said, "I will build my church" (Matt. 16:18). The evangelism, discipleship, church planting, and church growth aspects of home or foreign missions deserve the attention of the most qualified people in the church of Jesus Christ.

The author of this book has three essential qualities that merit attention today. First, he has been a successful church planting missionary for over thirty-six years. There is no substitute for experience in this area. Second, he has taught this subject from his experiences with lay people in Portugal to graduate classes of students from many countries and continents around the world. The depth of his knowledge in this area has brought invitations from different countries to lecture. Third, the subject of church planting involves principles and lifestyles that are borne out of the Scriptures and applied in daily life. There is a big gap between an academic apprehension of the evangelistic and church growth principles inherent in this book and a lifestyle of godliness and personal relationships. The author reflects these virtues, and they breathe in his writings.

Dr. Faircloth is esteemed in Europe as one of the outstanding post-World War II evangelical missionaries. He sailed to Portugal in 1949 under the Conservative Baptist Foreign Mission Society. I suspect that he represents the same "North American syndrome" of many of us in serving as missionaries in Europe: We were going to get the job of evangelizing a country accomplished within ten or fifteen years using high-powered methods we had witnessed in North America. In differ-

11

ent ways, places, and times we discovered that missionary endeavor is hard work. We had to learn that ministry involved more than importing the newest evangelistic fad that had surfaced in America or anywhere else. By the late 1950s this realization had brought American missionaries working in Europe around to a solid, biblical program of church planting and its long-term results, based upon the agenda of the New Testament. It is the biblical and strategic vision behind this book to focus attention upon planting churches which will, in turn, possess the dynamic to reproduce themselves in other churches.

In 1983 the author was assigned to me as a doctoral candidate preparing his thesis at Trinity Evangelical Divinity School. His outstanding academic background and practical skills were undergirded by a mind disciplined by engineering training at the University of Illinois. Probably his own father, a manager in an engineering manufacturing company, contributed to the management principles and sensitivity to detail reflected in this book.

Another important contribution to this book is the human factor related to a profound and certain call to the evangelistic and missionary ministry. Even after ministry in Portugal, his preparation of this book has been strengthened by five years of teaching a multi-cultural student body at Tyndale Theological Seminary and by ministry in the world-class city of Amsterdam.

Dr. Faircloth deals with the subject of church planting in a thorough way, yet he is sensitive to the cross-cultural applications of God's work around the world. He has written as a giant in his own right who also possesses a humble and gentle heart. These qualities should give permanence to this book over decades to come.

Arthur P. Johnston, Ph.D.
Tyndale Theological Seminary
Badhoevedorp, The Netherlands

Preface

World evangelization is proceeding at a pace unprecedented in the history of the church. Peoples in every corner of the globe are targets of evangelistic thrusts. Missionary evangelists take advantage of an awesome array of communication methods and devices which seem to increase daily. Such missions strategists as Dr. Ralph Winter dare to project the completion of the task of reaching the remaining people groups by the year 2000!

In the midst of the elaboration of strategies and the pressures of evangelism itself, there is an urgent need to stop and analyze what is going on. In the sending countries and in many target areas overseas, churches with long histories are obviously in difficulty. It is not unusual these days for pastors and local church leaders to admit that they do not really know what is the matter. There are all kinds of excuses and mutual accusations. Students who come from all over the world to better prepare for Christian ministry in our new seminary in Amsterdam confess without hesitation that local churches in their countries are not adequately fulfilling their biblical missionary responsibility. Missiologists Donald McGavran, David Hesselgrave, and others have focused attention on the fundamental necessity to concentrate missions strategy on the planting of literally millions of local churches throughout the world. Given the obvious condition of many churches in our day, however, this is easier said than done! The sad fact is that the spiritual blight which characterizes so many churches certainly threatens progress toward the goal of world evangelization.

My wife and I spent thirty-six wonderful years as missionaries to Portugal. We were heavily involved in a variety of educational and

evangelistic projects during those years. In so doing, we faced the enormous psychological "roadblock" which missionaries face in much of
the world today: We were among the precious few who really knew the
Lord, an evangelical population which at best did not amount to one
percent of the population. We too, like others of our colleagues, won-
dered why Portugal had not been evangelized after over a century of
dedicated missionary work. It is by no means unusual to say that we
learned many valuable lessons.

We observed churches in all stages of growth or non-growth. We
observed missionaries working in a wide variety of ministries. We initiated evangelism which resulted (unplanned and planned!) in new
churches. Our college and seminary classes forty-five years before had
not prepared us for church planting. We had never seen an American
church plant another church. Neither had we ever heard anyone speak
of the importance of doing it. We were forced to learn "on the job." We
learned that in evangelism it is not difficult to give birth to the "baby"
in the Portuguese scene. The real challenge lay in raising that baby to
become the right kind of "adult." How should one proceed? What
should an adult church look like—one that follows the Scriptures as
the only rule of faith and practice? Some thought that teaching people
to give financially was the great unmet need. Others thought that we
needed to teach people to do personal evangelism. Others emphasized
the mass distribution of literature, the education of more pastors and
Christian workers, or some other activity. However, the practical solution was always just beyond our grasp. What is the real goal of financial independence? To what end does aggressive evangelism serve?
What are we to educate more pastors and Christian workers to do?

In this book I have attempted to relate several things that we have
learned. First of all, it is imperative that the church planter understand
the final goal of each church planting effort and that he keep this
always in the forefront of his elaboration of strategy and employment
of methods. In the following pages this goal is precisely defined. Of
parallel importance are the principal parts or components of the final
goal. At this level one begins to understand more of what is really
involved in the planting of a New Testament church. This book, then,
seeks to dissect the church planting operation to discover what our
immediate, medium-, and long-range goals must be in order to reach
the identified final goal.

Furthermore, once ultimate objectives have become clear, it is necessary to delineate what has to be done in order to achieve each intermediate goal. It is not enough to be able to recognize the goals in
church planting. One must know how to proceed, given the individual
situation. This book places a heavy emphasis on balance throughout
the church planting process; without it, churches go off on tangents.

It is my sincere prayer that this book will not only be a text for classes in church planting and growth but also a reference text for church planters who are starting new works in the field. I am confident that it can also serve as an instrument for analyzing ailing congregations in any culture and for helping their leaders to correct the ills that keep them from healthy multiplication and growth.

Samuel D. Faircloth
Badhoevedorp, The Netherlands,
Winter 1990

PART 1

Introduction

1

The Missionary Burden

It would appear that the normal expectation in New Testament days was that the convert to Christ would associate with other believers in a new and unique kind of fellowship. It was a fellowship not only with other believers but also with God the Father and his Son, Jesus Christ (1 John 1:3). The early church knew little of isolated converts drifting from a local church fellowship. This brings me to believe that the express purpose of evangelists and apostles during the apostolic age was to see local churches planted in ever increasing numbers all over the known world. They were not occupied, as are so many today, with doing evangelism that took no practical thought of what would become of converts.

Spirit–Empowered Commission

This missionary burden for the planting of the church was born of the Spirit. Jesus shared the prophetic pattern for his world mission in Acts 1:8. Robert Coleman states the goal: "He intended to save out of the world a people for Himself and to build a church of the Spirit which would never perish."[1] It is curious to note also that there was "no anxious appeal to Christians to spread the Gospel."[2] The Holy Spirit took charge of and empowered these early witnesses. They were able to obey

1. Robert E. Coleman, *The Master Plan of Evangelism* (Wilmore, Ky.: Asbury Seminary, 1963), 17.
2. Roland Allen, *The Spontaneous Expansion of the Church and the Causes Which Hinder It* (Grand Rapids: Eerdmans, 1962), 6.

the Great Commission (see Matt. 28:19; Mark 16:15; Luke 24:46–49, and John 20:21) only in the power of the Holy Spirit. The book of Acts has been entitled by many "The Acts of the Holy Spirit": "Acts is governed by one dominant, overriding and all-controlling motif. This motif is the expansion of the faith through missionary witness in the power of the Spirit. . . . One hardly knows where in Acts to look for a distinction between Church and mission. Restlessly the Spirit drives the Church to witness, and *continually churches arise* out of the witness."[3]

To attempt to comply with our Lord's commission in the energy of the flesh is to doom the effort to failure. The church will be confused and discouraged. There can be no doubt, however, that the will of the Holy Spirit is the continuous planting of new churches throughout the world.

Spirit-Impelled Witnesses

As in the church of Thessalonica, the joy of the Holy Spirit experienced in true conversion to Christ causes a congregation to "sound forth" the Word of God to new places (1 Thess. 1:6, 8). True believers in our churches become *witnesses*, just as the early Apostles and believers. Where the Spirit is in charge, effective witness to Christ will result. A missionary statesman reminds us that, in relating to the world, the fundamental mission of the church is to witness of the saving grace of God to all men and in so doing "*to plant churches which will multiply themselves* and extend the witness of their living Lord."[4] This simply means that the marching order which our Lord gave to his disciples in Acts 1:8 ("you shall be my witnesses") is built into every true Christian. The urge to share the good news accompanies a new nature indwelt by the Holy Spirit. The Spirit impels witness.[5] The Apostle Paul's letter to the Corinthians expresses his personal burden and that of every Spirit-filled Christian. He said, "For if I preach the gospel, I have nothing to boast of, for I am under compulsion; for woe is me if I do not preach the gospel" (1 Cor. 9:16). To the Christians in Rome he wrote, "I am under obligation both to Greeks and to barbarians, both to the wise and to the foolish" (Rom. 1:14).

Spirit-Gifted Community

The inevitable result of this spontaneous, Spirit-filled witness was the planting of new local churches.[6] A new believer feels a need to

---

3. Harry R. Boer, *Pentecost and Missions* (Grand Rapids: Eerdmans, 1961), 161. Emphasis author's.

4. Melvin L. Hodges, *A Guide to Church Planting* (Chicago: Moody, 1973), 18. Emphasis author's.

5. Allen, *Spontaneous Expansion*, 9–10.

6. Ibid., 7.

meet others who share his or her new found faith. I believe that it is a spiritual burden for fellowship. They want contact with "those who have received a faith of the same kind as ours" (2 Pet. 1:1). Certainly one of the basic convictions that leads me to write this book is that it is not only desirable but imperative that evangelism, resulting from any method, be accompanied by firm purpose to see converts joined together in a local, disciplined church fellowship (Acts 14:19–23).[7] It seems to be the contention of most serious students of the missionary enterprise that such fellowship, nurtured, gifted, and moved by the Holy Spirit, will result in a motivation to grow and to establish other new churches. Missiologist David J. Hesselgrave expressed it well when he said that the primary mission of the church and, therefore, of the churches *"is to proclaim the gospel of Christ and gather believers into local churches where they can be built up in the faith and made effective in service, thereby planting new congregations throughout the world."*[8]

The Goal: Adulthood

This inherent urge to see new congregations come into being is not only the result of the Spirit's ministry in Christian converts; it is also explained within another analogy—that of adulthood. Even though our society consists of many childless marriages, the very existence of the human race depends upon what we may legitimately call the normal adult experience. It is expected that normal adulthood will issue in the birth of new lives. Birth control schemes practiced in third world countries are often strongly opposed by couples who have children, even at the risk of the penalties for disobedience to the law. Having children is part of normal adult life.

How does this relate to church planting? Normal New Testament Christian experience is to make disciples, to win converts, to have a family, and to gather this family in a common bond. This is precisely what the apostles and their successors did. Experience teaches us that evangelism in a missionary framework without reproduction becomes a dead end. It can be compared to an olympic relay race in which a runner fails to pass the baton to the next runner: the race is thereby stopped! In Christian circles such failure could be rightly considered to be corporate selfishness and disobedience. Those who truly love the Master obey Him (John 14:21). Those who obey the Lord Jesus make disciples, baptize them, teach them and gather them into local fellowships as the Apostles did. In a healthy spiritual community this process

---

7. Ibid. See Adolf Harnack's comment regarding the first three centuries.
8. David J. Hesselgrave, *Planting Churches Cross-Culturally: A Guide for Home and Foreign Missions* (Grand Rapids: Baker, 1980), 20.

repeats itself along the lines of Hesselgrave's "Pauline Cycle" (see figure 1)[9] and Paul's exhortation to his coworker Timothy (2 Tim. 2:2). I will maintain in this book that the planting of new churches is the natural preoccupation of adult congregations. Such congregations demonstrate certain characteristics which will occupy our attention in the following chapters.

Today's Challenge

We are always encouraged by the fact that "Jesus Christ is the same yesterday and today, yes and forever" (Heb. 13:8). The Holy Spirit also continues his ministry in and through the Church. Missionaries on the cutting edge of evangelistic endeavor in modern times face the challenge of *modus operandi*—how to proceed. Theological students, missionary appointees, and veterans in the field have approached me with this practical question: What would you advise me to do in a given situation? Finding answers is a challenge to ingenuity.

This question, faced by earnest servants of the Lord the world over, is occasioned by several factors. Unfortunately there often is a certain spiritual paralysis in the sending churches which are not planting new churches at home. Missionaries are sent out who have never seen a church planted and have never participated actively in planting one. Likewise, numerous educational institutions in the sending countries often provide excellent biblical and theological preparation but are woefully lacking in training for a solid church planting ministry at home or abroad.[10] This deficiency is being corrected in a number of schools around the world. Then, of course, missionaries are often bewildered as they face the need to adapt their approach through strategy, planning, and methodology to the cultural frame of the target people. It has been extremely useful to me to consider ways in which some missionary leaders have come to grips with approach. Recent innovative publications by men of experience are extremely useful to help church planters determine how to solve their problems. The following are brief introductions to their material.

The Pauline Cycle

One of the most widely used publications today is *Planting Churches Cross-Culturally*, by Hesselgrave, a former missionary church planter in Japan. The author calls attention to "the logical elements in Paul's mas-

---

9. Ibid., 59.

10. Donald A. McGavran, "Schools of Mission," *India Church Growth Quarterly* (Madras: Church Growth Association of India) 3 (July–Sept. 1981): 172. He writes, "passage through most seminaries almost guarantees a static-minded minister. He has been trained by professors who do not teach evangelism and plant no churches."

Fig. 1
"The Pauline Cycle"

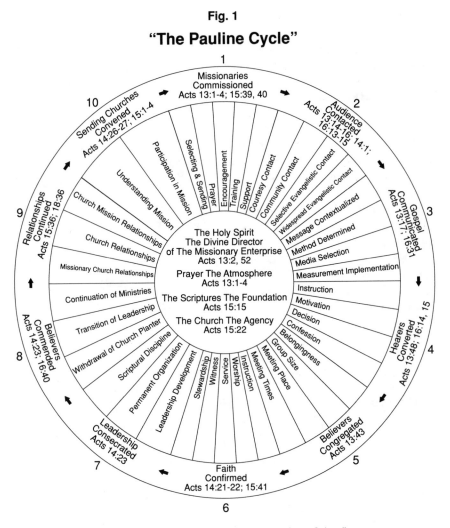

Adapted from David J. Hesselgrave, *Planting Churches Cross-Culturally:
A Guide for Home and Foreign Missions* (Grand Rapids: Baker Book House, 1980),
59, 136, 158, 200, 232, 270, 304, 350, 384, 402, 426.

ter plan of evangelism." Here he is obviously concentrating his analysis
on the elements of the church planting procedure to be found in Acts.
This "Pauline Cycle" (figure 1) is composed of ten elements:[11]

1. Missionaries Commissioned (13:1–4; 15:39, 40).
2. Audience Contacted (13:14–16; 14:1; 16:13–15).
3. Gospel Communicated (13:17–41; 16:31).

11. Hesselgrave, *Planting Churches*, 58.

4. Hearers Converted (13:48; 16:14, 15).
5. Believers Congregated (13:43).
6. Faith Confirmed (14:21, 22; 15:41).
7. Leadership Consecrated (14:23).
8. Believers Commended (14:23; 16:40).
9. Relationships Continued (15:36; 18:23).
10. Sending Churches Convened (14:26–27; 15:1–4).[12]

Hesselgrave stresses four characteristics of his Pauline Cycle. First, it gives direction to the church planting operation—there is a beginning and an ending. Second, even as they moved toward the end of the cycle in place, Paul and his team were involved in new beginnings in other places. Third, Hesselgrave observes that "the cycle must be viewed synchronically as well as diachronically." By this he recognizes that as a new work moves through the cycle, elements must continually be repeated. We must continue to seek new contacts and work for new conversions from the world even as we confirm the first believers in the faith. Fourth, the cycle is a standard by which to analyze churches that already exist, indicating where they might be "falling down on the job!"[13]

There can be no doubt that the ten elements of this cycle are basic activities taught and exemplified by the New Testament accounts and imperative for all successful church planting.

Obedience Oriented Teaching

It is George Patterson's conviction that "Biblical Church Extension principles, applied with methods compatible with the culture, should foster the spontaneous multiplication of churches in any mission field."[14] He has authored numerous publications in both Spanish and English, most of which are printed by the Honduras Extension Bible Institute. Patterson has worked with notable success in Honduras.

The William Carey Library published his most descriptive text-work-book, *Church Planting Through Obedience Oriented Teaching*.[15] His key word is *obedience*—obedience to Christ's commands. It is assumed that the population of the target area is reasonably receptive. Patterson's scheme of obedience oriented teaching takes TEE (Theological Education by Extension) one more step to become TEEE (Theological

12. Ibid., 61–63.
13. I have combined the ten figures of Hesselgrave's Pauline Cycle into a single figure for ready reference in figure 1.
14. George Patterson, *Applying Biblical Extension Principles* (La Ceiba, Honduras: IBE, n.d.).
15. George Patterson, *Church Planting Through Obedience Oriented Teaching* (Pasadena, Calif.: William Carey Library, 1981).

Fig. 2
Student-Teacher Communication

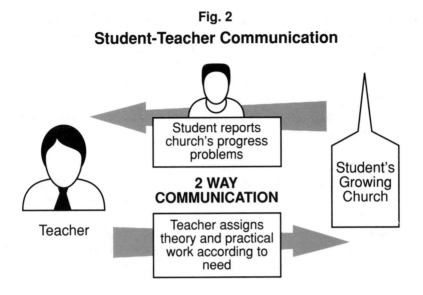

Student reports church's progress problems

2 WAY COMMUNICATION

Teacher

Teacher assigns theory and practical work according to need

Student's Growing Church

Education and Evangelism by Extension). Biblical education in an extension situation is thus made to serve evangelism and church planting. He says that, as Lord, Jesus Christ demands basic obedience in very specific areas within his church: (1) faith and repentance from sin, (2) baptism, (3) love, (4) the Lord's Supper (communion), (5) prayer, (6) giving, (7) witnessing.

Patterson claims that the whole church planting program succeeds or fails depending on the type of leaders who enroll in the training program.[16] Basic TEEE study units are detailed in this volume. We encounter church planting students who are guided step by step toward obedience to Christ's commands and taught to lead their new congregations in the same obedience. It is encouraging to hear that a growing number of theological schools throughout the world require a church planting internship for graduation. Graduates will engage in this important ministry if they are educated and encouraged to do so. Patterson encourages church planters working outside their own culture to adapt the basic seven points to their situations. Without doubt his TEEE system is innovative, and it has been successful in Honduras.

Seven Steps

Missiologist Donald McGavran, father of the church growth movement, suggests seven steps toward planting new churches. He expresses the scope of this missionary burden by observing that "any

16. Ibid., 3.

discipling of the peoples of the earth, of *all* the peoples of the earth necessitates aiming at establishing millions of new congregations. Carrying out the world mission of the Church is impossible, it is empty words, unless it rides on the back of multitudes of new congregations of the redeemed spreading through every ethnic and linguistic unit of mankind."[17]

McGavran's seven fundamental steps toward meeting this need can be summarized:

Step One—Pray and plan. In the sending church "prayer must begin in the pulpit." Planning must be bathed in prayer. "We need to carefully plan such a complex and difficult task as starting a new church."[18]

Step Two—Enlist helpers. Following Peter Wagner, McGavran suggests a goal of 10 percent involvement of the membership of those in the sending church whose lives have a good Christian testimony.

Step Three—Survey accessible areas. These should not be far from the sending church. Proximity, population trends, congregational contacts in the area, family web relationships, and family interest in Bible study are among items to carefully note.

Step Four—Evangelize whole families. McGavran emphasizes that Jesus exemplified this interest in Mark 1:29–31; Matthew 9:9–13, and Luke 10:38 and 11:37. Paul's ministry to families may be inferred from Acts 16:31–34 and 20:20.

Step Five—Find a place to meet. Starting with homes, a variety of possibilities present themselves, depending upon the local conditions.

Step Six—Begin meetings. Bringing believers together for worship, practice and obedience is the essence of a church. McGavran emphasizes that open Bible reading is basic to congregational meetings.

Step Seven—Train leadership. Each leader should be "someone the group respects and who is willing to give the many hours necessary."[19]

There is nothing new about these seven steps. They are part of the very core of reproductive ministry in church planting.

17. Donald A. McGavran, "Try These Seven Steps for Planting Churches," *Global Church Growth Bulletin* 18 (May–June 1981): 110. Emphasis McGavran's.
18. Ibid.
19. Ibid., 113.

New Churches Now

Possibly the most detailed "how-to-do-it" manual for planting new churches comes from Leonard P. Waterman, a home missionary experienced in starting churches in the United States.[20] Working in the context of a denominational mission society, Waterman edited a 276-page loose-leaf tool for training novices in church planting ministry for the USA. Eight sections, each accompanied by a helpful appendix, deal with principles and methods. Waterman identifies *fear* as a major reason why many young Bible school and seminary graduates hold back from involvement in planting new churches. The church planter in any culture can greatly benefit from such a manual.

Waterman calls attention to basic principles and suggests many practical ways to approach the task. A great deal of down-to-earth counsel is packed into sections covering establishing a basic outlook, determining the area, initial attitudes, relationships and qualifications, initial organization, housing, missions, developing the body, and setting up, recording and analyzing financial and numerical statistics.

Minute specifics of this manual are impressive. At least from the North American perspective, it ably meets the challenge for a *modus operandi*. Much of Waterman's counsel can be adapted to other cultures.

PERT (Program Evaluation and Review Technique)

PERT analysis originated in 1958 as a management system and was applied to the Polaris Missile System Program of the U.S. Department of Defense, by Lockheed Aircraft Corporation, the principal contractor. It has since become a widely used management tool. PERT "is a control instrument for defining the *parts* of a job and putting them together in network form so that the person responsible for each part and the man charged with overall management know *what* is supposed to happen and *when*."[21]

In about 1964, as B. J. Hansen was authorized by the government to publish *Practical PERT*, the Latin America Mission adapted its plan in graphic form in their booklet, *Evangelism-in-Depth According to PERT*.[22] Later, in 1971, the Mission Advanced Research and Communications Center (MARC) published the first edition of Edward R. Dayton's *God's Purpose/Man's Plans: A Workbook*: "This workbook discusses planning and goal setting as response to God's purpose for the

20. Leonard P. Waterman, *A Manual for Starting New Churches* (Wheaton, Ill.: Conservative Baptist Home Mission Society, 1979).

21. B. J. Hansen, *Practical PERT* (Washington, D.C.: America House, 1964), 10–11. Emphasis Hansen's.

22. Copies available from the Office of Worldwide Evangelism-in-Depth, Latin America Mission, Bogata, N.J. 07603.

Church and the individual Christian. A logic diagraming called PERT is described as a useful planning tool. A problem solving approach is discussed. Local evangelism is used as an example."[23] These publications are extremely helpful in understanding the PERT system and how it can be used.

In August of 1977, missionaries Paul and Agnes Sanders of the French field of the Conservative Baptist Foreign Mission Society, *Mission Evangelique Baptiste en France* (MEBF)—apparently drawing both from Dayton's workbook and Hesselgrave's Pauline Cycle—inaugurated an elaborate PERT system[24] to plant a church in Marne-La-Vallee. This plan projected the completion of the church planting operation there in approximately three years (July 1980), starting from zero. Reportedly the project went well.

My own experience with PERT planning extended from 1964 to 1970 while I was codirector for the national Evangelism-in-Depth strategy in Portugal, *Evangelização em Profundidade*. That exposure, together with seventeen years of church planting experience, led to an invitation in 1978 to teach a new course in church planting at *Instituto Bíblico Português*, the Portuguese Bible Institute of Greater Europe Mission (GEM). This course helped formulate the PERT system presented in this book. A general introduction to my application of PERT follows in chapter 2.

23. Edward R. Dayton, *God's Purpose/Man's Plans—A Workbook* (Monrovia, Calif.: Mission Advanced Research Center, 1978), i.

24. Two descriptive typewritten documents: "Planting a Church in Marne-La-Vallee" (25 pages) and "Overall Plans: Discussion Guide" (20 pages). Available through Conservative Baptist Foreign Mission Society, Box 5, Wheaton, Ill., 60189.

2

Management, Goals, and Planning Strategy

Management in Church Planting

"Is this spiritual or a carnal deviation from trusting the Holy Spirit? . . . Is it Biblical?"[1] Such questions are often raised in churches when management concepts are introduced. Edward R. Dayton and David A. Fraser prefer to call church management "planning in paradox. Here Christians take thought about (plan) everything, yet at the same time assume that God is at work in everything."[2] "The mind of a man plans his way, but the Lord directs his steps" (Prov. 16:9).

The need for sound management in the sphere of the life of God's people was anticipated by God himself. In the Old Testament era such managers as Moses and Nehemiah certainly demonstrated "divine wisdom" in handling what seemed to be insurmountable obstacles (Exod. 18:13–27; Neh. 2:11–3:32). In the New Testament era the Spirit of God has gifted men and women for management and administration of the life of the Church of Jesus Christ (Rom. 12:8; 1 Cor. 12:28). For this

1. Olan Hendrix, *Management and the Christian Worker* (Manila, Philippines: Living Books for All, 1972), 1.
2. Edward R. Dayton and David A. Fraser, *Planning Strategies for World Evangelization* (Grand Rapids: Eerdmans, 1980), 11.

Fig. 3

Management Functions and Activities

	Function	Activity
I	Management Planning	Estimating
		Establishing objectives
		Developing policies
		Programming
		Establishing procedures
		Scheduling
		Budgeting
II	Management Organizing	Developing organization structure
		Delegating
		Establishing relationships
III	Management Leading	Decision making (brainstorming)
		Communicating
		Motivating
		Selecting people
		Developing people
IV	Management Controlling	Establishing performance standards
		Performance measuring
		Performance evaluating
		Performance correcting

Louis A. Allen, *The Management Profession* (New York: McGraw-Hill, 1964), 68, reproduced in Olan Hendrix, *Management and the Christian Worker* (Manila, the Philippines: Living Books for All, 1972), 18–19.

reason management in church planting is a *spiritual* necessity that should not be taken lightly.

Management is defined as "the act or science of getting things done through other people,"[3] and as "the effective use of limited resources to achieve desired results."[4] A leading management researcher, Louis A. Allen, recognized by most experts in this field, makes it plain that management is work. He and others also emphasize that it is important to distinguish between *operating* or *technical work* and *management work*.[5] The manager must do both in the exercise of his duties.

3. Ibid., 26.
4. George L. Morrisey, *Management by Objectives and Results in the Public Sector* (Reading, Mass.: Addison Wesley, 1976), 5. Hereafter cited as *MOR*.
5. Ibid. See also, Dayton and Fraser, *Planning Strategies*, 26.

Management work involves planning, organization, leadership (which includes staff), and control. All the other assistance the manager renders to subordinates or to superiors is considered *operating work* and is normally of a technical nature.[6] What are the activities involved in these four managerial functions? Allen conceives of them as in figure 3 and says that "everything that is involved in any managerial situation can be plugged in under one of these four main headings or one of the nineteen sub-points. Everything!"[7]

Fig. 4

The MOR Funnel

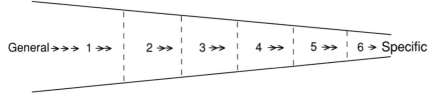

Allen, *The Management Profession*, 4.

Management by Objectives and Results

Management by Objectives and Results (MOR) is one of the established approaches to management. It has been ably presented in several publications since 1970 by management consultant George L. Morrisey. It requires the manager to focus on *results* rather than on *activities*.[8] It requires systematic planning, as Morrisey illustrates with the MOR funnel (figure 4). There are six separate steps in the MOR funnel:

1. defining roles and missions,
2. determining key results areas,
3. identifying and specifying indicators of effectiveness,
4. selecting and setting objectives,
5. preparing an action plan, and
6. establishing controls.

This system appears to be perfectly compatible with the PERT management system that will be used in this book.

6. Morrisey, *MOR*, 5–7.
7. Hendrix, *Management*, 19.
8. Morrisey, *MOR*, 2.

"As a process, MOR moves from the general to the specific. Its purpose is to subdivide a large complex effort until it reaches a manageable unit size."[9] Morrisey quotes Ed Green, who stated that "planning (management work) involves three things we don't want to do: (a) we have to think, (b) we have to do paper work, and (c) we have to use orderly procedures."[10]

> In essence, this approach breaks down the job of a manager into its basic functions and activities, selects those that are most important to effective management, and lays them out in a logical train which, if followed realistically, will almost inevitably lead to greater productivity and job satisfaction.[11]

A Circular Model

Dayton and Fraser present management for Christian mission as a process involving ten consecutive steps (see figure 5). These ten steps can be summarized as four:

1. Define the mission in terms of need.
2. Plan the mission.
3. Attempt the mission in the power of the Spirit.
4. Evaluate the mission with the mind of the Spirit.[12]

But how can we relate all of this to church planting? How can this process help us to think?

Application

Basic to management work is thinking, and thinking is not easy for any of us. It demands determined effort. Dayton and Fraser claim that "there are no born managers."[13] Church planters, though gifted by the Holy Spirit for administration, must be willing to develop this skill. Management is a *learned* skill.[14] Church planting, whether cross-cultural or national, should not be characterized by what Morrisey calls "seat-of-the-pants management."[15] Unfortunately, in the name of spirituality, much of the Lord's work is carried on in spur-of-the-moment

---

9. Ibid., 4.
10. Ibid., 8. Excerpted from a filmed address by Edward J. Green, "How to Manage Change Through More Effective Planning" (New York: American Management Association, n.d.).
11. Ibid., 15.
12. Dayton and Fraser, *Planning Strategies*, 42.
13. Ibid., 43.
14. Ibid., 27. Emphasis author's.
15. Morrisey, *MOR*, 3.

Fig. 5
The Planning Model

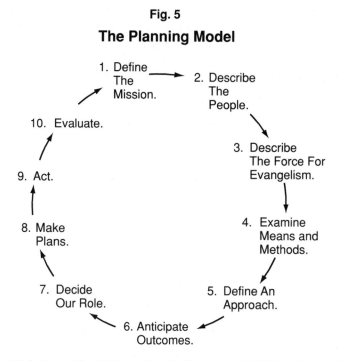

Edward R. Dayton and David A. Fraser, *Planning Strategies for World Evangelization, 43.*

fashion, lacking predetermined objectives. Careful thinking, bathed in sincere prayer and dependence upon the leading of the Spirit, often spells the difference between failure and success in a church planting effort. Perhaps more than any other ministry in the Lord's work, church planting merits the best in managerial skills. It is a fact that "the *absence* of planning is more likely to dampen the work of the Spirit than extensive planning."[16] In this chapter I am especially concerned with the function of management planning: How should the church planter begin to *think* about the ministry?

Goals Essential to Reproduction

Clear Goals

One of the most important aspects of planning—in fact, inseparable from the very concept of planning—is the setting of objectives, according to Olan Hendrix.[17] Clear goals give us great advantages. It is suggested that (1) clear goals strengthen communication, (2) clear goals

16. Dayton and Fraser, *Planning Strategies*, 29.
17. Hendrix, *Management*, 58.

are basic to good planning, (3) clear goals provide a basis for discussion and change, (4) clear goals help to show the direction of progress, and (5) clear goals strengthen and test our faith.[18] To guarantee clarity, all goals should be well written; they should focus on results, have a time limit, and be specific, practical, and feasible. A goal should state something *definite* we want to accomplish; we must be able to *measure* our success in achieving it. "Goal setting can be used as a way of reflecting our understanding of God's purpose for us as His Body."[19]

Church Planting Goals

Gene Getz, in introducing his excellent little volume, *The Measure of a Church*, expresses my own sentiments:

> This book has grown out of personal concern regarding my own work for Jesus Christ in the local church. It has grown out of a *deep concern* that I personally might do God's work in God's way, that I might have a philosophy of the ministry that is truly biblical, and that I might have both *proper goals at which to shoot* and proper criteria for evaluating my efforts.[20]

What are the *proper goals* for a church planting effort? What is the ultimate objective? The burden of world statistics, of which all of us are reminded in the media, emphasizes the great need to begin many more evangelical churches. Serious reflection about this need leads us to one overpowering conclusion: We must work in such a way that we motivate existing churches to reproduce themselves and we must plant new churches that have both a capacity and the resolve to reproduce themselves.

Church planting in any situation must make a high priority of the goal of *reproduction*—the multiplication of local churches throughout the land. Church planters must not be satisfied with the mere birth of an infant congregation. That goes as well for the establishment of a mission outpost or a preaching point. They must strive to reach the long-range goal of nurturing a mature adult congregation, one which will enthusiastically engage in planting other new churches. Dayton and Fraser set the parameters for this work: "The ultimate goal for evangelization is the creation of communities which will participate in evangelization."[21] "The ultimate strategy should always involve the formation of a dynamic church."[22]

18. Dayton and Fraser, *Planning Strategies*, 438–41.
19. Edward R. Dayton, *God's Purpose*, 9–14.
20. Gene A. Getz, *The Measure of a Church* (Glendale, Calif.: Regal, 1975), 9–11.
21. Dayton and Fraser, *Planning Strategies*, 333.
22. Ibid., 311.

Several years ago, C. Peter Wagner challenged my thinking in *Frontiers in Missionary Strategy*.[23] He defined a mature church, not as self-supporting, self-governing, and self-propagating, but as one that . . .

1. lives for others,
2. can take care of itself, and
3. is relevant to its cultural situation.

In the chapters that follow I will accept these three subgoals as constituent parts of the overall goal—a mature, reproducing congregation.

To better understand what is meant by overall goal and subgoal, the reader might wish to take a quick preview look at the fold-out PERT chart, "How to Plant a Church Capable of Reproducing Itself," enclosed with this book. Each of the bewildering sets of lines and boxes will be sorted through in due time, but for now, let us focus on the right side of the chart, where all those steps are headed. Box 44 is the final or overall goal—a new, mature, adult church, able to reproduce itself. That will not happen, however, until three subgoals are achieved: The church must exist for others, and not be merely a self-contained entity (box 41). Of course, the subgoal of self-sufficiency—being able to take care of itself (box 42)—is also necessary. Another vitally important subgoal is the church's willingness and ability to communicate personal love and the gospel dynamically—relevantly—in its cultural situation (box 43). Other subgoals contribute to making these subgoals a reality.

In discussing these "subgoal" characteristics of maturity, Wagner gives nine further suggestions which help us to understand what each of the three actually stands for.

In the first place, a church that exists for others has two outstanding characteristics: It is sensitive to the felt social needs of the community and reaches out to people in true Christian love and concern; it also actively engages in church planting in neighboring communities as well as in world missions to other lands and cultures. In the second place, a church that can take care of itself will do so psychologically, liturgically, spiritually, administratively, and financially. Sufficiency in all five constituent areas must be reached in order to have a church that takes care of itself. In the third place, a church that is relevant to its cultural situation demonstrates "one of the most advanced signs of maturity."[24] Certainly such a church is acclimated to the culture of the area, and it is experiencing in its evangelism conversions from the

---

23. C. Peter Wagner, *Frontiers in Missionary Strategy* (Chicago: Moody, 1971), 163–67.
24. Ibid., 167.

world. A church cannot be sealed off from its surroundings and at the same time be the agent of reconciliation that God intends it to be. Cultural relevance is essential to effective communication of the message.[25]

Of course, as a church planter begins his ministry, his first major objective is to plant the baby congregation, step five in David J. Hesselgrave's Pauline Cycle (figure 1). Wagner, who served as a missionary in South America, is rightly concerned with what will happen to that baby! I likewise found that to be my major concern while planting churches in Portugal. My conversations with church planters from Uganda, Zaire, Central African Republic, Nigeria, and Zimbabwe as well as from Korea, the Philippines, Japan, Thailand, and India reveal similar interest.

How to Proceed Using PERT

Strategy

One of the most difficult things to do, observes Hesselgrave, is to "get out of old ruts and chart new paths."[26] Richard B. Cook wrote of Paul that

> he worked in an *orderly way* from Jerusalem as far as Illyricum (Rom. 15:19)—around the Mediterranean coastline to the Adriatic. The team stayed for months at a time in one province or area (1 Cor. 16:5–8), but once the gospel had been "established" (not preached, Rom. 15:19) and house churches had been founded, Paul felt there was no longer "room" (Rom. 15:23) in these regions.[27]

Cook calls Paul "the disciplined, intentional strategist."[28]

Modern missionary literature presents a wealth of helps for church planters working on strategy, such as Edward R. Dayton and David A. Fraser's outstanding contribution, *Planning Strategies for World Evangelization*. Their premise is:

> In one sense everyone and every organization has a strategy or strategies, a way of approaching a problem or achieving a goal. . . . A strategy is an overall approach, plan, or way of describing how we will go about reaching our goal or solving our problem.[29]

25. David J. Hesselgrave, *Communicating Christ Cross-Culturally* (Grand Rapids: Zondervan, 1978), 106–16.

26. Hesselgrave, *Planting Churches*, 79.

27. Richard B. Cook, "Paul, the Organizer," *Missiology* 9 (Oct. 1981): 488. Emphasis author's.

28. Ibid.

29. Dayton and Fraser, *Planning Strategies*, 15–16.

As Christians we have a tremendous advantage in considering strategy. Because we have the Word of God, a source of ultimate values and absolutes, we can most appropriately develop *grand strategy.* . . . Our role is to cooperate with him in bringing his kingdom to fruition.[30]

As in the MOR system, church planting strategy moves from the general to the specific and concentrates on results. Our final felt need or goal—the ultimate result—is *a mature church capable and motivated to reproduce itself.* Yet we cannot focus on that one need alone. Other results must be achieved first to make the final goal attainable. A cross-country hiker contemplating a long trek over mountainous terrain never forgets the point of destination. Neither can he forget individual mountains and rivers that lie along the way. Daily provisions, climbing equipment, and other gear must be carried so the walker will not run out of food in the short-run, nor fail to surmount the immediate challenge of a cliff.

The same applies to this journey. We require what Dayton and Fraser call a *grand strategy* to map out a path to the final goal. We know what sort of church we want. How do we propose to achieve it? To confront individual challenges and contribute to final success we must also develop an *intermediate strategy*—measures that will achieve elements crucial to the whole. These are the subgoals we have already met, plus a number of others detailed on the complete PERT chart. Finally, effective planning requires a third breakdown of intermediate strategies into more minute objectives or components—a *short-range strategy.*[31]

Planning with PERT

PERT is described by B. J. Hansen as "a control instrument for defining the parts of a job and putting them together in network form."[32] Dayton calls it "a useful planning tool."[33] The reader already has glanced at the complete PERT system we propose, but we will begin with a simplified version, found in figure 6. Two definitions are central to understanding PERT terminology. Each numbered box represents a goal or step to be achieved, which is called an *event*. Steps or events related to one another are connected by lines in the same way a hiker's map shows the path between successive points to be reached. Each set of solid lines indicates a chain or *network* of activities and events to be planned to reach the next major goal. The subgoals these events influence are shown by broken lines.

30. Ibid., 19. Emphasis author's.
31. Ibid., 313–14.
32. Hansen, *Practical PERT*, 10–11.
33. Dayton, *God's Purpose*, i.

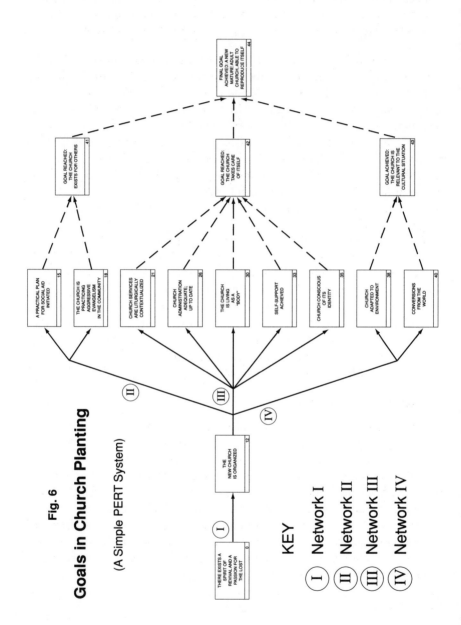

Fig. 6
Goals in Church Planting

(A Simple PERT System)

THERE EXISTS A SPIRIT OF REVIVAL AND A PASSION FOR THE LOST — 0

Ⅰ

THE NEW CHURCH IS ORGANIZED — 12

Ⅱ

Ⅲ

Ⅳ

A PRACTICAL PLAN FOR SOCIAL AID INITIATED — 15

THE CHURCH IS PRACTICING AGGRESSIVE EVANGELISM IN THE COMMUNITY — 18

CHURCH SERVICES ARE LITURGICALLY CONTEXTUALIZED — 21

CHURCH ADMINISTRATION ADEQUATE, UP TO DATE — 26

THE CHURCH IS LIVING AS A "BODY" — 30

SELF SUPPORT ACHIEVED — 33

CHURCH CONSCIOUS OF ITS IDENTITY — 35

CHURCH ADAPTED TO ENVIRONMENT — 38

CONVERSIONS FROM THE WORLD — 40

GOAL REACHED: THE CHURCH EXISTS FOR OTHERS — 41

GOAL REACHED: THE CHURCH TAKES CARE OF ITSELF — 42

GOAL ACHIEVED: THE CHURCH IS RELEVANT TO THE CULTURAL SITUATION — 43

FINAL GOAL ACHIEVED: A NEW MATURE ADULT CHURCH, ABLE TO REPRODUCE ITSELF — 44

KEY

Ⅰ Network I

Ⅱ Network II

Ⅲ Network III

Ⅳ Network IV

It is important to read a PERT plan from left to right. In figure 6, on the extreme right, event 44 represents the final objective—a mature church able and motivated to reproduce itself. All activities and events in the whole plan will move from left to right in the direction of event 44. To the immediate left of event 44 are its three composite parts —events 41, 42, and 43. Notice that their relationship to the final goal is indicated by the broken line. On the extreme left event 0 represents hearts (of a church, a team, or an individual) prepared by the Holy Spirit with a will to evangelize and engage in church planting. This, of necessity, must be the beginning point of every church planting effort.

I noted earlier that a mature church has three characteristics which are integral parts of the final goal: events 41 (the church exists for others); 42 (the church takes care of itself), and 43 (the church is relevant to its cultural situation). Contributing to these are ten other events: 12 (the new church is organized); 15 (a practical plan for social aid is initiated); 18 (the church is practicing aggressive evangelism in the community); 21 (church services are liturgically contextualized); 26 (church administration adequate; up to date); 30 (the church is living as a "body"); 33 (self-support achieved); 35 (church conscious of its identity); 38 (church adapted to its environment), and 40 (conversions from the world).

The PERT system presented here seeks to order the ten goals so as to show their "logical" relationship to the three (41, 42, 43) and to the final result (44). This logical arrangement of the goals is made in the form of four *networks* with their respective subnetworks. In PERT planning each event or goal is preceded by the activity necessary to achieve it. In this way, each PERT network or chain consists of *activities* and *events* along the way to a major goal in the plan.

Network I

In the figure 6 chart the network I chain of activities and events will terminate with the organization of a new infant congregation—event 12, our first major goal. This congregation can be compared to a newborn baby. For any church planter to think that his responsibility ends at this point is a gross error! This is especially true in a country with few sound evangelical churches. Normally, babies desperately need adult love and attention.

Network II

A special word of explanation is in order regarding networks II, III, and IV. These are not to be seen as consecutive. Network III does not follow network II; network IV does not follow network III; rather they all simultaneously follow network I. Hesselgrave's remark that the Pauline Cycle "must be viewed synchronically as well as diachronically"[34] is very appropriate for this PERT system. Converts will continue to come to the Lord, be baptized,[35] be discipled and be congregated. Likewise, in networks II through IV progress toward the stated goals will be subject to local conditions. Various activities will be repeated, will overlap, or will be carried out simultaneously with varying degrees of success.

The chain of activities and events in network II is directed to achieve event 41—a church that exists for others. Within this chain, however, are two subnetworks, each with its own goal. One set of activities initiates a practical plan to meet social needs of the community, insofar as possible—event 15. Other activities practice aggressive evangelism in the community and nurture support for world evangelism—event 18. Once a church has begun to show concern for both physical and spiritual needs of others, it can be considered to be living for others. The broken lines connecting events 15 and 18 to 41 indicate this relationship. The events are so interrelated that achieving both 15 and 18 means reaching 41.

Network III

Network III has five important subnetworks, graphically located in the center area of the figure 6 PERT plan. Again the church planter understands that reaching the five subordinate goals automatically achieves another major goal—a church that takes care of itself—event 42. If the church is to attain this objective it must (1) effectively communicate the Christian message in its liturgy or form of worship, (2) adequately administer its own affairs, (3) live as a "body," (4) become financially self-supporting, and (5) be truly conscious of its own identity or be psychologically well-adjusted.[36] These five objectives—in figure 6, events 21, 26, 30, 33, and 35—contribute in a powerful way to the maturity of the local church.

Network IV

The chain of activities in network IV has been divided into two subnetworks in order to point out two closely related aspects of cultural relevance that jointly achieve event 43—a major goal in the plan. One subnetwork concentrates on making sure that the church is adapted to its environment—event 38. The other aims at winning converts from the surrounding non-Christian world—event 40. The close relationship

---

34. Hesselgrave, *Planting Churches*, 62.

35. See the complete PERT Chart. Activity 44, which is not described in our text, graphically reminds us that new baptisms will continue to take place throughout the life of the church.

36. See Wagner, *Frontiers*, 164, for references to Tippett, Beyerhaus and Lefever on this point.

between the goals of network IV and those of network II can readily be perceived.

Possible Objections

In the following chapters I will systematically develop the complete PERT plan for church planting advocated in this book. It does not pretend to be the last word in church planting strategy. My thinking regarding this plan is analogous to that of Hesselgrave on his Pauline Cycle. He admits that "the whole thing seems too tidy to be true, too programmatic to be practical. . . . there is nothing sacrosanct about this particular way of breaking the task down into manageable elements."[37]

The purpose of this thinking-through of the process is to alert church planters around the world, especially those working among mostly unevangelized people, about what is involved in truly fulfilling their task. In many areas the multiplication of new churches through the efforts of existing churches is the crying need of the hour. We can hardly afford to plant new churches which have little or no missionary vision to repeat the operation.

In relating any generic strategy to an immediate local situation, I agree with Dayton and Fraser that "every situation we face is different, that each one requires its own special strategy."[38] The PERT plan presented here must be adjusted, altered, and amplified where necessary to settle upon the "unique solution strategy"[39] deemed wise and necessary in each church planting situation.

37. Hesselgrave, *Planting Churches*, 58.
38. Dayton and Fraser, *Planning Strategies*, 18.
39. Ibid.

PART 2

The Preparatory and Pioneer Periods

3

The Preparatory Period

Spontaneous Expansion

Activity 00: The Holy Spirit revives the life of the church individually and collectively, resulting in a profound love for the Lord, for one another and for a lost world without Christ (figure 7).

Fig. 7

The Spirit Revives

The Spirit Revives

Conversations with national evangelical leaders reveal a growing preoccupation with the need for a missionary vision in the churches. "Why," they ask, "is the primary mission of the church being largely neglected when the need is so great?" This question is a matter of utmost importance, and the neglect of our mission is depriving multitudes in every nation from hearing the message of eternal life in Christ.

Roland Allen focused upon *spontaneous expansion* in the early church, as indicated in Acts 8:4 and 16:5 and in 1 Thessalonians 1:8:

> This then is what I mean by spontaneous expansion which follows the unexhorted and unorganized activity of individual members of the Church explaining to others the Gospel which they have found for themselves; I mean the expansion which follows the irresistible attraction of the Christian Church for men who see its ordered life, and are drawn to it by desire to discover the secret of a life which they instinctively desire to share; I mean also the expansion of the Church by the addition of new churches.[1]

A former colleague and missionary to Portugal, Arthur S. Brown, likewise moved by the burden for more new churches, wrote that the need today is two-fold. *"First,* our churches need to experience a revival that 'whole church evangelism' fosters. *Second,* they need to sense anew the divine purpose for their very existence."[2] Although this is true, there is yet a prerequisite—the kind of revival which Stephen F. Olford describes as *preceding* evangelism. Revival, Olford observes, "is a strange and sovereign work of God through which He visits His people, *restoring* them, *encouraging* them and *freeing* them for the fulness of His blessing. Such a divine intervention will *result* in evangelism even though, *first of all,* it will be a work of God in the Church and in each believer."[3]

The Holy Spirit and the Pentecost event stood absolutely at the beginning of the history of the New Testament church. It is from the Spirit that the life of the church is derived.[4] The Spirit and the Spirit alone confers life. Olford's heart-cry is for a renewal of this life in the church, without which she is impotent and even disinterested in evangelism. A local congregation must "walk by the Spirit" (Gal. 5:16). There needs to be a revival of this walk that the church might heartily engage in conferring spiritual life to others (2 Cor. 3:6–12). Without spiritual cleansing and renewal a local church cannot profitably embark on any program of evangelism and church planting.[5] In fact, present experience seems to prove that such a church will not even attempt to do so.

Spontaneous expansion in the New Testament era undoubtedly took

1. Roland Allen, *The Spontaneous Expansion of the Church and the Causes Which Hinder It* (Grand Rapids: Eerdmans, 1962), 7.

2. Arthur S. Brown, *How One Church Can Start Another* (Conservative Baptist Foreign Mission Society, 1957), 5.

3. Stephen F. Olford, *Heart Cry for Revival* (London: Marshall, Morgan and Scott, 1963), 17. Emphasis Olford's.

4. Harry R. Boer, *Pentecost and Missions* (Grand Rapids: Eerdmans, 1961), 98–99.

5. See Oswald J. Smith, *The Man God Uses* (London: Marshall, Morgan and Scott, 1932). Also excellent in this regard is Lewis Sperry Chafer, *He That Is Spiritual* (Grand Rapids: Dunham, 1965; repr. ed., Grand Rapids: Zondervan, 1974).

place with the power and immediate intervention of the Holy Spirit who moved the Church to witness (Acts 1:8). For this fundamental reason, as we think our way through network I of the PERT plan for the planting of a new church we must first seek the divine renewal of Spirit life in those who will do the work.[6] I am convinced that church planting is on the very cutting edge of missionary activity. It can only be successfully entered upon in the power of the Holy Spirit, no matter who initiates the action.

The Initiative—Whence?

Activity 0 (Goal: event 1): The Holy Spirit causes his servants to desire to plant a new church, whether an individual, a church, a mission society, or a denomination (figure 8).

Fig. 8

Divine Initiative

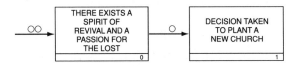

A survey I conducted in Portugal of more than seventy churches in eight different denominations and groups revealed that 74 percent began through the initiative of a pastor or licensed church worker. Six percent resulted from the initiative of the elders of another local church. Sixteen percent resulted from the initiative of other members of a church, whereas four percent were the fruit of the initiative of persons other than area church members. It would be extremely interesting to have more details about exactly what happened in the planting of hundreds of new churches in the first century. For instance, who took the initiative to give a witness in Colossae? Was it an individual from Colossae who found the Lord elsewhere? Was it an apostolic team? A traveling businessman? Another existing Christian assembly nearby? That there existed a witness through a profusion of common Christian believers there can be no doubt. The New Testament (for example in Acts 8:4 and 1 Thess. 1:8) and other early historical records[7] indicate a spontaneous expansion. The Spirit moved through the Roman world and extended the gospel witness to the western extremities of the known world well within a century of the event of Pentecost.

6. F. Jack Redford, *Planting New Churches* (Nashville, Tenn.: Broadman, 1978), 30. The climate in the mother church must be conducive.

7. Allen, *Spontaneous Expansion*, 7.

How we long to see more of this initiative in today's world! Could it be that few are listening to the Spirit's voice? Melvin Hodges issues a clarion call to Christians to individually and corporately hear and obey:

> Our part is to follow the divine initiative. To bring this about, believers must be filled with and controlled by the Spirit. Care must be taken to give heed to divine guidance . . . (Acts 8:26) . . . to the divine will . . . (Acts 10).

> The activity of the Holy Spirit is *not confined* to the evangelist or the church planter. The whole church is the temple for the dwelling of God by the Spirit (1 Cor. 6:19–20). The Spirit desires to dwell in the whole church and to direct *all* of its members and not the ministers only.[8]

The burden for church planting is truly born of the Spirit. This then is basic to a sound decision to open a new work.

The Church Planting Team

Activity 1 (Goal: event 2): Review biblical principles of leadership (figure 9).

Fig. 9
Qualifications for Church Planters Established

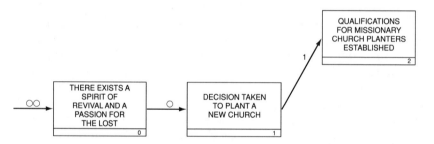

Once the decision has been made, preferably by a church as a whole, to plant a new church, attention must be given to the question of whom the Spirit would have to lead this new ministry. Remember that the ultimate goal in this section of network I is to have a church planting team prepared for action (PERT chart, event 4).

Just what is the profile of an ideal church planter? Surveys of both missionaries and nationals, made in consultation with church planters in Portugal, show how opinions can differ on this matter. I asked the following questions and received the responses noted:

---

8. Melvin L. Hodges, *A Guide to Church Planting* (Chicago: Moody, 1973), 26–27. Emphasis Hodges's. This book is an excellent commentary on the Holy Spirit's work in expanding the church.

1. Does a church planter need a special call of the Lord for this work? Sixty-three percent answered, "Yes."
2. Should he have had previous pastoral experience? Fifty-four percent answered, "No."
3. Should he have completed formal theological and biblical studies? Fifty-four percent answered, "Yes."
4. What level of secular education should he have achieved? Fifty percent said this was not important; 38 percent said a high school education or the equivalent is desirable, whereas 12 percent said a university education is needed.

Even though it is important for local churches *as churches* to become involved in starting new churches, practical considerations and experience also demonstrate that first the pastor or some key elder will be moved by the Spirit to take action. This leader will eventually attract others who are also moved by the Spirit to cooperate (Acts 13:1–4). The church planter *par excellence*, according to New Testament records, was the Apostle Paul. His testimony in 2 Corinthians 6:1–10 reveals some basic characteristics fundamental to his success. Alfred Plummer rightly relates that Paul "points the way in which an Apostle [a missionary church planter?] does his work and what he has to endure."[9] First, the Apostle Paul was a coworker—a team man—and at the same time a servant of God.[10] Second, he was careful not to cause offense and discredit the ministry. Third, in the face of a wide variety of adverse experiences and persecution, he was able to endure. Fourth, as a Spirit-led and controlled person, fruit (purity, patience, kindness, love) was evident in his life .

Hodges[11] and also Leonard P. Waterman[12] give some very useful suggestions concerning the person of the church planter. I have listed these for ready reference in figure 10.

A church planter must certainly possess the qualities of a leader. LeRoy Eims asks, "Who is fit to lead?" Not everyone! Not everyone qualifies as a church planter. Why? Because not everyone looks to God and to him alone for *sufficiency*. Not everyone lives a *pure life* (2 Tim. 2:19–21). Not everyone is a *humble* servant of God (1 Pet. 5:5–6). Not everyone comes to God in *faith* (Heb. 11:6).[13]

9. Alfred Plummer, *Second Epistle of Paul to the Corinthians* (Edinburgh: T. & T. Clark, 1915), 189.
10. Ibid. Plummer helpfully comments that the context permits three objects which could grammatically complete the Greek participle of v. 1 that is translated, "working together with": (1) God—2 Cor. 5:18, 21; (2) Christ—2 Cor. 5:20; (3) you—the Corinthians.
11. Hodges, *A Guide*, 28–31.
12. Waterman, *A Manual*, 97–104.
13. LeRoy Eims, *Be the Leader You Were Meant to Be: What the Bible Says About Leadership* (Wheaton, Ill.: Victor, 1975), 26–39.

Fig. 10
Qualifications for a Church Planter

Qualifications	Descriptions
Natural Qualifications	1. Socially and educationally acceptable to the people to be reached. 2. An outgoing personality. 3. Seriously, sincerely interested in people with deep concern for their personal problems. 4. Ability in public speaking. 5. An attractive personality. 6. Exemplary family life.
Spiritual Qualifications	1. A heart given totally to God. 2. A deep and abiding compassion for the lost—sacrificial devotion (Luke 15:3–7); patient persistence in seeking out the lost (Luke 15:8–10); one who never gives up (Luke 15:11–32). 3. A life of continual prayer (Col. 1:9–11; 2:1–3; Eph. 3:14–19; Matt. 9:38). 4. A life utterly dedicated to the work of the ministry. 5. A highly motivated vision—one who will see possibilities and not obstacles.
Attitude toward self	1. Certainty—of God's call. 2. Honesty: confidence in God; willingness to learn from more experienced persons; understanding that new Christians must be taught scriptural new-church principles. 3. Responsibility.
Attitude toward the new nucleus of believers	1. Acceptance toward those who have defects. 2. Openness toward those who have positive gifts he may not have. 3. Spiritual determination. 4. Patience, understanding, love.
Attitude toward the community	1. Positive attitude (Acts 18:9–10). 2. Anticipation. 3. Friendliness. 4. Acceptance.

Adapted from Melvin L. Hodges, *A Guide to Church Planting* (Chicago: Moody, 1973), 28–31 and Leonard P. Waterman, *A Manual for Starting New Churches* (Wheaton, Ill.: Conservative Baptist Home Mission Society, 1979), 97–104.

With these important preparatory considerations taken into account, a church is ready for event 2 in our PERT plan.

Activity 2 (Goal: event 3): Prayerfully select members of the church planting team (figure 11).

Fig. 11

Team Member Selection

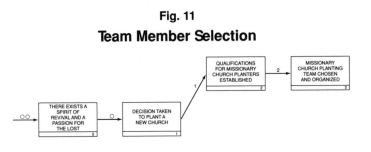

Sixty-eight percent of the church planters interviewed in Portugal reported that they had worked with a team to begin new churches. Moreover, 85 percent of these worked with the support of their local church or local churches. Many students of the New Testament church readily conclude from the Acts and Epistles that Paul "was the leader of a team of missionary organizers."[14] On this team were spiritually gifted coworkers. Richard B. Cook claims they practiced what he calls a "division of labor" working in "an orderly way."[15]

David J. Hesselgrave emphasizes that New Testament missionaries were not volunteers; they were willing but *chosen*—selected by the Holy Spirit through prayer.[16] The *Lord* thrusts forth laborers (Matt. 9:38; Luke 10:2). Any local church that proposes to plant a new church must look to the Lord in believing prayer that he might effectively select and enable those who should form the team. One of those so chosen will probably become the leader. Around him will gather those who are missionary minded, spiritually minded, concerned with the salvation of the lost, possessed of a team spirit, eager to work for God, capable of leadership at different levels, and optimistic, warm, loving, and caring. Those fit together will work in harmony because they desire to cooperate with the Lord in the ministry of reconciliation. How will the church know who these people are? God will speak to the

---

14. Richard B. Cook, "Paul, the Organizer," *Missiology* 9 (Oct. 1981): 487. The author claims that Paul was "a leader of a disciplined team of workers who traveled together and probably lived together in community as they moved from place to place."

15. Ibid., 487–88. See also David W. Shenk and Ervin R. Stutzman, *Creating Communities of the Kingdom* (Scottdale, Pa.: Herald, 1988), 42–55, for an excellent survey of New Testament teamwork.

16. Hesselgrave, *Planting Churches*, 142–44.

people and to the church. As in Acts 13:1–4, the task of building the team must be a delicate balance.[17]

Granted that the local church in question is experiencing spiritual revival (event 0), the Lord himself can be counted on to accredit those who will fill the various capacities as a team. These can then be joyfully commissioned by the local assembly to fulfil the ministry of planting a new church.

> *Activity 3 (Goal: event 4):* Prepare team members specifically to achieve church planting goals (figure 12).

Fig. 12
Team Preparation

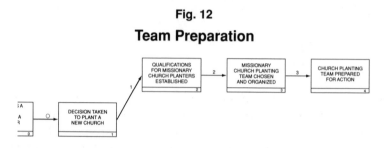

Since the whole church is to become involved in one way or another in supporting the team, the church planting goals shown in figure 6 should be carefully explained to the team and also to the entire body. This will inspire cohesion and foster unity fundamental to efficacious prayer and cooperative support (Phil. 2:2). This orientation could extend over several weeks. Once a church has had experience in church planting and is accustomed to *think* church planting, the training of possible future team members becomes a normal part of the lifeflow of the congregation. On-the-job training in different facets of church administration and organization is accepted, ongoing work in such congregations. Their eyes are on the harvest. For instance, new teacher candidates work with regular teachers in the Sunday school, expecting to eventually participate in outreach. These candidates may live in areas where new work is contemplated. This head start anticipates the actual decision to move into the area.

Leaders and Laity

Hesselgrave helpfully points out two types of training he sees occurring in Scripture. The team leader or leaders need special training. If the pastor is to lead, he will probably need to train himself through study and prayer. "Timothy and Titus were not trained in the same manner as were the saints at Berea [and] Thessalonica."[18] On the other

17. Ibid., 139.
18. Ibid., 151.

hand, the laity today can often take advantage of extension courses offered by Bible institutes and seminaries. This advanced-level training, properly administered, becomes a great training source for future team members.

Initial Essential Tasks

On our PERT plan (see complete chart), once event 3 has been reached, a list of initial essential tasks should be determined. These will include personal evangelism, area survey work, discipling ministries, and child evangelism. Those team members who will become involved in one or more of these tasks should receive instruction necessary to prepare them for action. Time should be taken for adequate preparation. I have personally taken advantage of parachurch organizations experienced in such ministries as child evangelism. They have helped to train people for specific ministry. The first time around always is the most difficult and takes the most effort.

The Target Area

Activity 4 (Goal: event 5): Choose possible target areas for a new church (figure 13).

Fig. 13
Target Area

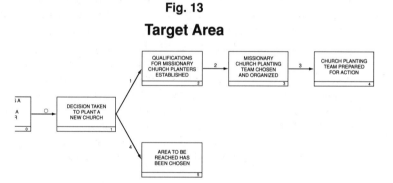

When we examine Christ's words in Acts 1:8 we can agree with Hesselgrave that "it seems that in most cases, a world vision is required to win our Jerusalems."[19] This means that the kind of true evangelistic vision that took our Lord Jesus to the cross (John 3:16) will be a *world* vision. A congregation with this vision will see far beyond the immediate area. I feel that this vision will become a reality in a Spirit-filled church. The Spirit is vitally interested not only in the nearby area but in the nation; not only in the nation but in the peoples beyond. World missions are the goal of the Spirit as he fulfills Christ's prediction in John 16:7–11.

19. Ibid., 94.

Local churches are at the center of his mission to reach their Jerusalems, their Judeas, their Samarias, unto the remotest peoples of the earth. As in Paul's day, so today cities are becoming more and more important. As rural people migrate to cities for economic and sociological reasons urban centers "do present the greatest potential and possibilities for planting churches. This is due to: (1) openness to change, (2) the concentration of resources, and (3) the potential for significant contact with surrounding communities."[20] The rapidly accelerating growth of the world's cities is a fascinating phenomenon which is attracting the attention of evangelical strategists the world over. This book cannot focus on the dynamics of this challenging fact. Others are becoming authorities as to the statistics and in the approaches evangelism and church planting should take in world-class cities and urban evangelism in general.[21]

Even though missionary church planters are being sent out from local churches to the remotest peoples of the earth, a Spirit-filled congregation cannot sit back and think that missions begin beyond the country's borders. A church that is on fire for the Lord in its burden for planting new churches must set priorities as to where to begin new work. Determining target areas within range of the local congregation is of great importance.

Many commendable factors can rightly or wrongly influence the selection of a target community. First, some Christians may already live there. This has led to unwise decisions, especially in countries where there are few churches and a need for better strategy. Second, believers may want their home communities evangelized. This is commendable, of course. I have seen several churches planted rather quickly where believers had a positive Christian witness. Third, people from that place may be asking, even begging, evangelicals to come. I remember one town where we were engaged in planting a new church. The reception was enthusiastic, and towns some distance away heard of what was happening. A delegation was sent from one of them insist-

20. Ibid., 100. Those working in church planting in "world-class cities" should consult a growing volume of literature on this by men such as Ray Bakke, Tim Monsma, Harvie Conn, Roger Greenway, Ralph Neighbor, and David Barrett.

21. F. Jack Redford, although speaking to the local North American scene, has posed some questions to guide churches in the selection of target areas. They are listed in the appendix. One of the most extensive compilations of ideas and materials for selecting the target area that I have found, also geared to North America, is found in Waterman, *A Manual*, 37–94. A number of other materials are mentioned in Orrin D. Morris, dir., *Surveying New Communities to Establish New Churches* (Atlanta: Research Division, Home Mission Board of the Southern Baptist Convention, 1981), as well as in F. J. Redford, *Evangelizing and Congregationalizing* (Atlanta: Home Mission Board S.B.C., 1977); *Church Community Needs* (Atlanta: Home Mission Board, 1980); David J. Hesselgrave, *Planting Churches*, 93–100, and Ezra Earl Jones, *Strategies for New Churches* (New York: Harper & Row, 1976), 77–86.

ing that we come. We could not do so then, but later a vital work was begun in the town that had so desired it. Fourth, the place is socially or economically strategic and geographically accessible to a local church.

As a rule, *accessibility* is extremely important to church planting that arises from an existing local church. If we want the whole church involved, the new work must be within reach. If the team is from the local church, accessibility becomes even more essential. In one church planting project in Portugal the new work was five kilometers away. When public meetings were finally possible in the target area, dozens of people from the planting church accompanied the team on Sunday evenings to bolster attendance at the new work. In another place a number of visitation teams from the base church were able to easily travel to the target community Thursday nights to help the team with the initial contact ministry. In both cases the accessibility was crucial to the support received from the greater body of the congregation. It amplified the enthusiasm for planting new churches. Members were able to give themselves to the work!

One denomination which is growing rapidly in a country in southern Europe and leads the field there in church planting has used another rather unusual strategy. They may move several key families, who have been formed into a team, into a more inaccessible unreached target area for the purpose of planting a church. Although far from other local churches, this work is supported in prayer and with occasional visits by lay leaders and ordained ministers. In this way key cities can be penetrated even though far from existing churches. A number of Christians working together encourage one another during the early hostile reception they might receive. It takes great dedication to find new employment and move one's family to a new location. Spirit-led believers are able to do this with joy and great satisfaction.

Activity 5 (Goal: event 6): Make a detailed demographic survey of the target area (figure 14).

Fig. 14
Demographic Survey

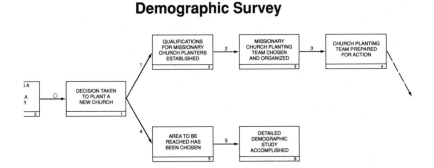

Ezra E. Jones distinguishes between what he calls "the general area survey" and a "feasibility study":

> The former is much broader than the latter. The general area survey covers a large geographical area including many neighborhoods. It is done for the purpose of working out a general denominational strategy for ministering to the area. It is a broad survey using specific data to establish general guidelines for future decisions. The feasibility study, on the other hand, is limited in most cases, to one particular community or segment of the larger area originally surveyed. It is for the specific purpose of determining whether a new church is needed and, if so, the right time for launching it. The feasibility study will also take into consideration the larger ministry of the denomination in the area but only with regard to how it affects and is affected by the decisions regarding a new church in a specific community.[22]

Activity 4 would certainly involve a church in some sort of general area survey. However, once a preferred target area has been decided upon (event 5), a far more detailed study of the selected area is in order. This, perhaps, would include a feasibility study. I have placed a useful list of fourteen specific questions Jones suggests for such a study on p. 184.[23]

Also note F. Jack Redford's "Community Profile" and his "Area Analysis for Church Extension" (see pp. 187–89).[24] The former covers the community, the people, and the churches, whereas the latter seeks religious, population, economic, and institutional data. Hesselgrave has a concise suggestion for an overall profile of a potential target community which is included on pp. 191–94.[25]

An indispensable item in demographic survey work is an area map showing the exact area and composition of the target community. The availability of detailed information will depend on local government records. City, county, town, and village planning commissions will often make available data on residences, businesses, parks, roads, zoning, and future plans. Studies of businesses, corporations, telephone companies, and power and light companies may also be available; this is invaluable information.[26]

Some of this information, especially regarding industrial zoning, is vital to target area selection and would be part of Jones's general area survey. Once all demographic information has been gathered and evaluated, the final decision can be made more confidently. In my survey of church planting procedures in Portugal, I discovered that 85 percent

22. Jones, *Strategies*, 87–88.
23. Ibid., 89–90.
24. Redford, *Planting*, Appendices A and B.
25. Hesselgrave, *Planting Churches*, 101–4.
26. Ibid., 100.

of the new churches were planted without demographic studies. I believe the Lord's work merits more attention to detail than that. For examples of excellent demographic work, see Ralph W. Neighbour, Jr.'s, studies of Brisbane, Australia, and Brussels, Belgium.[27]

   Activity 6 (Goal: event 7): Elaborate the initial evangelistic strategy for the target area (figure 15).

Fig. 15

Initial Evangelistic Strategy

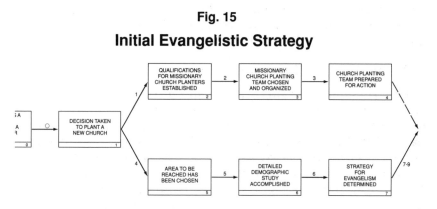

Perhaps it should be unnecessary to emphasize the need for an initial strategy for evangelism. Even under the guidance of the Holy Spirit, the most effective means must be discerned by looking at the situation. In countries where such sects as Jehovah's Witnesses and Mormons have become increasingly active once-successful canvassing methods are being reevaluated by a number of national church planters and missionaries. How should we enter an area which knows little or nothing of the evangelicals and their message? Ken Stephens, a successful American pastor, observes that in New Testament-era evangelism both individual and mass approaches were used. "Situations, opportunity, and time determined which method was used."[28]

Preevangelistic Courtesy Contacts

   Perhaps, as a part of a demographic survey procedure, the team should make what Hesselgrave calls courtesy contacts, calling upon government leaders, officials, and mass-media representatives.[29] The motive is obvious: create good will and open doors for the new work (see Pauline Cycle, figure 1).

27. Ralph W. Neighbour, Jr., *Brisbane: Resistant or Neglected?* (Ferny Hills, Queensland: Touch International Ministries, 1987); idem, *Baptist Strategy Report (Brussels)* (Brussels, Belgium: Belgium Baptist Mission, 1983).
28. Ken Stephens, *Discipleship Evangelism* (Scottsdale, Ariz.: Good Life, 1978), 25.
29. Hesselgrave, *Planting Churches*, 166–67.

Limited Area Canvass

In spite of the bad reputation of the sects in this technique, it may be advisable to plan for a systematic limited area canvass. I have found this to be one of the useful ways to find open doors for personal evangelism. The team should determine how many contacts they can deal with at a time. Then, as this predetermined number is reached, the canvass should be suspended and evangelism initiated with those interested. If people are contacted and show interest and then are not followed up immediately, they very likely will be "turned off" to any future attempt to deal with them.

An Informative Approach

This is called *preevangelistic community contact* or "getting to know the people in the community and allowing them to know us."[30] In many areas a high percentage of the population has never had any personal contact with an evangelical. In Roman Catholic lands this is especially true. Many are victims of slanderous, libelous propaganda disseminated over the past centuries by priests and hierarchy. Therefore, some missiologists advocate enthusiastically that evangelical churches plan their own propaganda penetration into such areas to explain our real beliefs about God, the Trinity, the Bible, Mary, the saints, and the church. In this way we might open the door for evangelism.

Mass Contact

The Assemblies of God have used large tents, erected in strategically located lots in the target community. Hodges comments that there are several ways to initiate a campaign: "The evangelist may hold an open-air campaign on a piece of ground which he has leased for a few months of a year. He may pitch a tent, erect a temporary structure, or simply build a platform and set up lights and a public address system."[31]

Arthur S. Brown combines elements of the above strategies. The area should be canvassed by two-person teams who distribute a printed invitation to meetings and a gospel tract. Evangelistic meetings of one or two weeks should then be held in a rented building which he recommends should be the future home of the expected new congregation. He stresses that "the choice of the building is very important to the success and to the future of the work."[32] Mass contact may not be wise in some cultures, however, especially in the initial thrust.

30. Ibid., 169.
31. Hodges, *A Guide*, 34.
32. Brown, *How One Church*, 18.

Meetings in Homes

"House churches" have been the center of evangelism from New Testament times. Such strategy, however, assumes that there is a contact either with Christians living in the area or sympathizers who will open their home. As far as the financial outlay is concerned, this would appear to be a most practical way to begin.

A survey of sixty-nine churches planted in Portugal reveals that 38 percent started in homes, 28 percent began in a hall either rented or loaned, 9 percent were the result of open–air meetings, 9 percent resulted from literature distribution, 7 percent grew out of evangelistic campaigns and another 9 percent began through various other ways.

Selective Evangelistic Contacts

Hesselgrave advocates the prayerful selection of initial evangelistic contacts. He fears that merely reaching the most readily available may identify the emerging church with converts who are considered "undesirables" by the larger unsaved community. This suggestion merits serious consideration. Hesselgrave writes that church planters must consider carefully the target culture and its social dynamics when planning initial evangelistic contacts.[33]

Whichever plan is finally decided upon, some suitable strategy for efficient discipleship of each new convert should also be included as an essential part of the plan.

33. Hesselgrave, *Planting Churches*, 173.

4

The Pioneer Period

Evangelism in the Target Area

Activity 7 (Goal: event 8): Execute the initial evangelistic strategy in the target area (figure 16).

Fig. 16

The First Converts

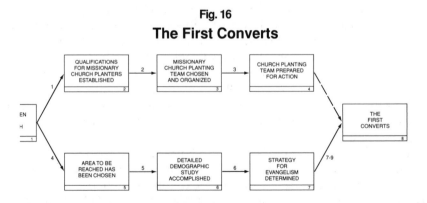

By this time, if the previous actions have been undertaken, the Holy Spirit normally has generated enthusiasm and expectancy in the congregation and in the team members. No matter which initial evangelistic strategy has been decided upon, a local church caught up in this kind of missions expects God to act and looks forward to blessing in the target area. Preparatory steps, bathed in believing prayer and demand-

61

ing dedication and sacrificial service from the whole church exhilarate a congregation that is reaching specific goals for the glory of God.

Nevertheless, several factors will tend to determine how many members of a local church actually participate in the initial effort. For one thing, in most cultures, the working day is rather long. It may be due to a longer lunch hour. Few men in the city can be free before 9 p.m., and many times it is even later for those living in the country. The economy is such that families need more than one job in order to subsist. This problem can be partially solved by giving attention to the scheduling of evangelistic activities to avoid impossible situations.

Second, if the target area is not within easy reach of the home congregation, those who have no transportation are eliminated unless other arrangements are made. Planning can anticipate this.

Third, if a *determined effort* is not made to involve as many of the local congregation in evangelism as possible, the team will be left with the entire load. Well-intentioned pastors and church leaders must stop haranguing church members about their need to do personal evangelism. Rather, they should actively *involve* as many as possible in definite goal-oriented ministry that employs their spiritual gifts in positive service. We must stop complaining that people do not serve the Lord and devise ways that will help them into service!

Effective Communication: The Objective

The *heart* of our task at this point must be evident to each one who participates in evangelism: the effective communication of the gospel in the target area.[1] If non-Christians are to understand the good news, repent of their sin, believe in Christ and enter into the fellowship of a new community with others of like faith, what shall *we* do in collaboration with the Holy Spirit? Charles Brock, who has had a measure of success in the Philippines, says in his volume, *The Principles and Practice of Indigenous Church Planting*, that church planters "must deliver the Christian message in the native context of thought." Such a worker "goes to people who have thoughts and philosophies strange and different from his."[2]

Biblical doctrines must be put into language the local national can understand. The chart in figure 17 is one tool useful in the process of communicating to just about any local context, whether Buddhist, Hindu, Muslim or animist. To accurately fill in the right side of the chart you need to converse about these subjects with those you are seeking to evangelize. We have found answers simply by interviewing people

---

1. David J. Hesselgrave, *Planting Churches Cross-Culturally* (Grand Rapids: Baker Book House, 1980), 199. See biblical precedents in John 3 and 4; Acts 13:16–17; 17:2–3; 9:20–22.

2. Charles Brock, *The Principles and Practice of Indigenous Church Planting* (Nashville: Broadman, 1981), 48.

Fig. 17

Audience Orientations in Relation to the Christian Message

Religious Orientation: nominal Christian (Roman Catholic)
Percentage of Target Community: 94 percent.
Basic Beliefs:

Central Biblical Doctrines	Predominant Beliefs of the Target Audience in Portugal
1. *God:* Creator, Sustainer of Universe; a personal being who has will, is moral and holy, reveals himself to man, demands worship, condemns idolatry . . .	*God:* There is no God, or there is a supernatural force over everything, or there is a personal creator God who hears prayers, perhaps, who might be interested in man.
2. *Man:* Created by God in his image; a fallen creature; the object of God's redeeming love . . .	*Man:* The highest animal. Some men want to do right and some are bad. Man can build a better world and a better life if he will.
3. *Jesus Christ:* Preexistent; fully God and fully man: incarnation; Lamb of God; substitutionary death . . .	*Jesus Christ:* A good man killed by bad men. Or Jesus was God but they killed him; he was a martyr.
4. *Sin:* Rebellion against God's will; true moral guilt entailing judgment and resulting in estrangement and death . . .	*Sin:* Vague understanding as some wrong thought or act against society or God. Only practicing Roman Catholics would perceive it as being rebellion against God's will.

David J. Hesselgrave, *Planting Churches Cross-Culturally* (Grand Rapids: Baker Book House, 1980), 226. Adapted to Portugal here.

selected at random on the street. Questionnaires designed to collect information about what people think or believe can be locally designed by the team or obtained from such organizations as Campus Crusade for Christ. These brief interviews can result in an evangelistic contact.

"Real communication does not occur until the message is both comprehended and acted upon by the recipient as intended. Communication, in reality, is a two-way process," according to James F. Engel.[3] In our experience in southern Europe, the legitimate meanings of such biblical terms as "new birth," "born-again," "confession," "salvation," "prayer," and "saint" had to be clarified. In the Roman Catholic context throughout the world, this is more necessary than ever since Vatican Council II. Roman Catholics are now open to study the Bible with us, and many are eager to do so. It is essential to keep this two-way process in mind, no matter what the religious framework. For example, in contextualizing the message for Roman Catholics, it is good to remember the Lausanne assessment of the Roman Catholic scene:

> Many Catholics have a superficial understanding of basic Christian doctrine. They give intellectual assent to the truths of Jesus' person, work, and nature. They believe in the existence of sin, but are unclear as to its practical implications. They admit that they are sinners, but guilty only of "little" sins. They may have no clear concept of heaven and hell, and are convinced that man will be saved by his good works. Many feel that holiness as taught by Roman Catholic doctrine is attainable only by the "saints." They recognize that God exists. He is creator of the universe, but is remote and disinterested in human affairs. They may fear his punishment and often seek to placate him in ways mixed with superstition. They may see no need for a personal relationship with him.[4]

The *vehicle* of effective communication, wherever we are attempting to plant the church, must be a practical demonstration of a caring, loving, sensitive perception of the felt needs of the people we are trying to reach. Our example is of utmost importance, as Paul reminds us in his letter to the Philippians (3:17; 4:9).

Methods of Communication

Although some methods of communication will be more appropriate to a context than are others, church planters I have interviewed concur that we offer as much variety as possible. Having said that, the most popular in many cultures today is preaching or Bible study in the homes of believers or friends. David J. Hesselgrave says such methods

---

3. James F. Engel, *How Can I Get Them to Listen?* (Grand Rapids: Zondervan, 1977), 15.
4. Lausanne Occasional Papers, *No. 10: Thailand Report—Christian Witness to Nominal Christians Among Roman Catholics* (Wheaton, Ill.: Lausanne Committee for World Evangelization, 1980), 10–11.

as visitation evangelism and small-group Bible studies "allow for true dialogue in which the respondents have the opportunity to share their opinions and ask questions, and the missionary-evangelist has a chance to relate the gospel to the specific needs of the respondents."[5] Brock adds:

> The worldwide popularity of the Bible inclines the people to be open to a study of its contents. . . . It is wise for the planter to make very clear his immediate objective and the nature and content of the study. Even unbelievers appreciate open honesty. . . . This gospel (Good News) is most clearly seen in a study of the Gospel of John.[6]

The Holy Spirit and Conviction

According to John 16:8, the conviction of sin, righteousness and judgment is the ministry of the Holy Spirit. Only he can convict men of the sin of not believing in the Savior. Only he can convict men that Jesus' righteousness is uniquely sufficient for their acceptance by the Father. Only he can convict men that Satan is judged and man can be saved from his dominion. Therefore, as we evangelize we must touch upon these themes while sharing the gospel with others. In this way, we collaborate with the Spirit in his special ministry. It is in this power of the Spirit that we can persuade those in the target area to accept Christ as personal savior.

Activity 8 (Goal: event 8): Take careful note of the spiritual decision process while evangelizing (figure 16).

This is one more activity which concentrates on the achieving of goal or event 8 in our PERT strategy—the winning of the first converts. One of the most helpful ways to relate the principal parts of the Great Commission (Matt. 28:18–20) is the so-called "Engel Scale" shown in figure 18.[7] It is a noteworthy attempt "to place the communication ministries (proclamation, persuasion and cultivation) in the perspective of the spiritual decision process that is followed as one becomes a believer in Jesus Christ and grows in the faith. . . . It depicts the interactive role of both God and the human communicator in this process."[8]

Each participant in the initial evangelistic strategy and everyone engaged in the various methods used would do well to study this scale and be aware of what is happening in God's role, his or her role as a

---

5. Hesselgrave, *Planting Churches*, 224.
6. Brock, *Principles and Practice*, 72.
7. First suggested by Viggo Sogaard and later revised and popularized by James F. Engel. See also Engel, *How to Communicate the Gospel Effectively* (African Christian, 1988).
8. James F. Engel and H. Wilbert Norton, *What's Gone Wrong with the Harvest?* (Grand Rapids: Zondervan, 1975), 44.

Fig. 18

The Spiritual Decision Process

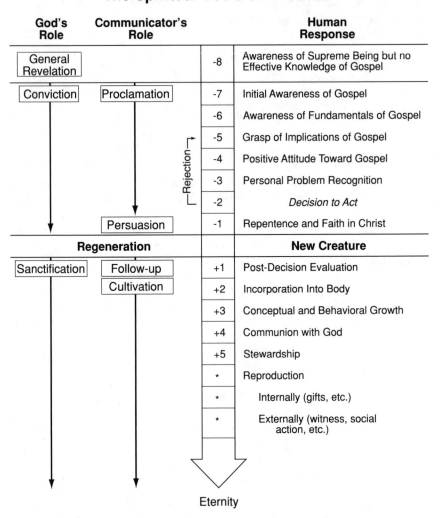

God's Role	Communicator's Role		Human Response
General Revelation		-8	Awareness of Supreme Being but no Effective Knowledge of Gospel
Conviction	Proclamation	-7	Initial Awareness of Gospel
		-6	Awareness of Fundamentals of Gospel
		-5	Grasp of Implications of Gospel
		-4	Positive Attitude Toward Gospel
		-3	Personal Problem Recognition
		-2	*Decision to Act*
	Persuasion	-1	Repentence and Faith in Christ
Regeneration			**New Creature**
Sanctification	Follow-up	+1	Post-Decision Evaluation
	Cultivation	+2	Incorporation Into Body
		+3	Conceptual and Behavioral Growth
		+4	Communion with God
		+5	Stewardship
		*	Reproduction
		*	Internally (gifts, etc.)
		*	Externally (witness, social action, etc.)

(Rejection applies to levels -5 through -2)

Eternity

James F. Engel and H. Wilbert Norton, *What's Gone Wrong with the Harvest?* (Grand Rapids: Zondervan, 1975), 45. This model was suggested by Viggo Sogaard, a student of Wheaton Graduate School, and revised by Engel and published in the *Church Growth Bulletin* and other publications. It was improved by Richard Senzig of the faculty of Wheaton Graduate School and by C. Peter Wagner and Charles Kraft of the faculty of Fuller School of World Mission.

communicator, and in the process of the response of the one evange-lized. By taking careful note of the spiritual decision process illustrated in figure 18 the evangelist will avoid hasty superficial conclusions that could actually defeat the whole process.

Personal evangelism, as well as mass evangelism, runs the risk of falsely assuming that someone has become a believer because the person agrees to pray with the personal worker or evangelist. Signing a decision card does not make one a Christian. Praying with someone has been known to be a safe way of dispatching the evangelist! Gospel tract presentations such as the *Four Spiritual Laws* should be used with Engel's Scale in mind. What is this person's true awareness of God and the gospel? God the Holy Spirit's role is to convict, moving the person to repentance and faith in Christ. Many times this takes time and cannot be accomplished in a twenty-minute conversation that consists of simply reading "cold turkey" through a tract or booklet. The evangelist's role is to be sensitive to the Holy Spirit and to clearly communicate the biblical message. Make sure that those doing the evangelism understand this. In fact, it will not be out of order to repeatedly counsel personal workers to beware of insisting on hasty "decisions."

Activity 9 (Goal: event 8): Make certain that each new convert has the proper counseling at the time of decision (figure 16).

It is difficult to separate evangelism from counseling. In our PERT strategy, activities 7, 8, and 9 are closely related in practice. A variety of excellent materials are available from Christian publishers to aid the spiritual counselor when dealing with a newly-born babe in Christ. The first hours of life are extremely important to both the one "born of the flesh" and the one "born of the Spirit"![9] A new believer must be assured by the Word of God of his new life in Christ (1 John 5:11–12).

First, regardless of how or where evangelism takes place, the one doing the post-decision counseling should visit the new "convert" in his home or at a suitable place within a day or so. Second, the counselor should pray with the convert. Third, biblical counsel and help should be provided insofar as possible. Fourth, the counselor should guide the student through the first lessons in personal Bible study. Fifth, the church planting team should be informed and their prayer solicited for this individual. Sixth, at the proper time the person should be encouraged to become part of a group of new Christians; it is good if the counselor personally accompanies the new believer to the group.

Central to the counselor's task is to make sure that this new believer has truly experienced biblical conversion (has turned to the Lord from former life and belief). Three key New Testament passages are important in describing conversion: Acts 3:19 and 26:18 and 1 Thessalonians 1:9.[10]

---

9. Evangelists generally claim that the first forty-eight to seventy-two hours after profession of faith are crucial. Most follow-up systems are built on this conviction.

10. Hesselgrave, *Planting Churches*, 233–34. The author has a valuable treatment of the whole conversion process (231–67). See especially "decision as a point and process," 250.

Christian Fellowship and Nurture Cells

Activity 10 (Goal: event 10): Gather the first converts for mutual edification (figure 19).

Fig. 19

New Believers Congregated

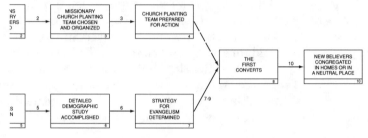

Perhaps one of the most exciting moments in church planting in a country where there are few Christians is when new believers are introduced to one another and begin to meet together. Figure 19 reminds us that it is imperative that new converts feel a part of God's family. They must feel togetherness with others of the same family. They must participate regularly in what the family is and does. This has proven to be a most significant experience of new Christians—the realization that they have a new family of people who really care about one another and can share their intimate needs from day to day. They did not have anything like this in the world.

The New Testament knows nothing of Christian believers living in isolation. Living in community with other believers is precisely what we as church planters should want to see happen to new converts. However, even though this is fundamental to reaching our goal, we must be sensitive to the immediate situation of each person. Very likely there are strong societal relationships and even community programs in which the person is involved. Some of these may be valuable in their own right. We must never pressure anyone into the group before he is able to take a stand on personal conviction.

Societal ties in local community organizations may take up the free time of their members. Sooner or later a new convert will be called upon to break with these connections in order to belong actively to the community of believers. While becoming a real part of this faith community, the convert should not be encouraged to so withdraw from other relationships that the witness for Christ is lost among those the believer knows best and has ready access to. In this circle is a wonderful opportunity to share with family and friends. I believe that the step of uniting with the believers will be a natural part of the decision *process*. Many times it will not be easy.

This does not negate the relative urgency to gather the first converts. Acts 2:42–47 can serve as a model at this point. By uniting new Christians in a local family community we accomplish several fundamental objectives: First, they become a mutual encouragement to each other; second, they cease to be isolated and lonesome in their newfound faith; third, they edify one another through prayer, Bible study and fellowship; fourth, they are more easily taught as a group which results in more efficient use of time for the church planting team; and fifth, they gradually form the nucleus of a new church, which we must always remember is our first major goal.[11]

In southern Europe we found that the first believers will most likely congregate in the home of one of the converts. This can be a problem unless both the husband and the wife are converted. In most countries, the average house will not comfortably accommodate more than eight or ten adults (ideal as a small group). This should not be considered a disadvantage, however. Several homes can be used simultaneously as the number of converts continues to grow. Some church planters advocate planting a "church" in *each* of the homes. This has been effective in such areas as the Philippines.[12] Del Birkey's recent book, *The House Church*, studies the apostolic and early Christian house churches. Without trying to argue against these valuable studies, I would advocate the advantage of grouping believers in several homes within a target area.

It will not be long before *all* the believers in the area will need to congregate regularly for corporate worship. Worship can already have occurred in the individual homes, as Birkey points out, and both Birkey and Brock forcefully argue that it is in the small gatherings where the initial strategy is implemented toward achieving our master goal—reproduction. Nevertheless, there is a certain strength and sense of greater support in a larger congregation. It must be admitted that in doing this we need to find a suitable place to accommodate everyone. Rental cost poses a formidable barrier. Purchase is out of the reach of new congregations. Foreign funds are not the answer for the overwhelming majority of church planting situations throughout the world. A more practical solution usually must be found.

In a variety of cultural backgrounds throughout the world, it seems to be a generally accepted fact that the local people identify the evangelicals with their places of worship. For this reason, nationals often feel that the place of meeting will either help or hinder the effectiveness of evange-

11. Melvin L. Hodges, *A Guide to Church Planting* (Chicago: Moody, 1973), 32–41.

12. Brock, *Principles and Practice*, 33. In the context of the United States, Lois Barrett, *Building the House Church* (Scottdale, Pa.: Herald, 1986), illustrates the process of planting house churches within the larger church. She provides a valuable bibliography of resources.

lism in the surrounding community. Under these conditions wisdom would seem to dictate that good taste be balanced with the actual potential of the local Christian believers. Buildings are not churches, and prestige is not the goal. "Keeping up with the Joneses" is not our goal either!

Discipling and Preparing for Baptism

> *Activity 12 (Goal: event 9):* Initiate a plan for discipling the new believers (figure 20).

Fig. 20

New Believers Discipled

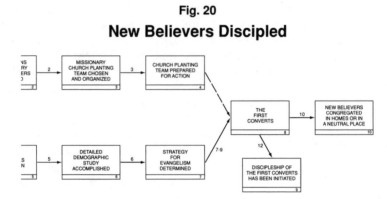

In figure 20 and the corresponding section of the complete PERT chart we are introduced to what is called a *supplementary network* of activities (12, 13, and 14) and goals (events 9 and 11). This sequence parallels or occurs in context with activities 10 and 11. Figure 20 shows the first step in this sequence, the discipling of new converts. Vergil Gerber affirms that "evangelism is changing people into disciples."[13] Jesus commands that "we make disciples of all the nations" (Matt. 28:19). Therefore, evangelism is a means to this end.

Gerber points out that a disciple is not only a *learner*, but is also a *servant* of his master-teacher with a commitment to obey him and his precepts (see figure 21). Therefore, Gerber said, the plan to disciple new believers implies both a commitment and a process.[14] In this sense "it is both an initial act and a continuing experience."[15] The disciple's lifestyle is changed. There are at least six areas to which the disciple of Jesus is committed. The highest commitment of all is to Christ (Luke 14:26, 27, 33). Other commitments are to the church (Acts 2:41), to obedience to the Word of God (John 8:31), to other members

13. Vergil Gerber, "Disciple" (an address given at the Consultation on Contemporary Evangelism, O'Hare Inn, Chicago, 30 Nov. 1976).
14. Vergil Gerber, *Discipling Through Theological Education by Extension* (Chicago: Moody, 1980), 38.
15. Ibid., 39.

Fig. 21
Commitment of Faith

Vergil Gerber, *Discipling Through Theological Education by Extension* (Chicago: Moody, 1980), 39.

of the body (John 13:35; Acts 2:44–45), to reproduce by winning others to faith in Christ (John 15:5), and to the worship and ministry of the church (Acts 20:7). Disciple making is the responsibility of every member of the church, for each member is also a disciple.[16]

The church planter who accepts PERT event 44 (a *mature* church, capable and motivated to *reproduce* itself) as the ultimate long-range goal must recognize "that to disciple in the context of the evangelistic mandate is to make responsible, reproducing *Christians* who in turn make responsible reproducing congregations."[17] It is not my purpose here to adequately deal with all the aspects of discipling and discipleship. An abundance of excellent, helpful literature is available today for church planters around the world.[18]

Activity 13 (Goal: event 11): Carefully teach the new believers the basic doctrines of the faith (figure 22).

Fig. 22
The First Baptisms

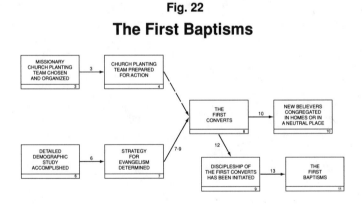

16. Ibid., 43–44.
17. Ibid., 46–47.
18. Suggestions besides Gerber's may be found in such sources as Walter A. Henrichsen, *Disciples Are Made—Not Born* (Wheaton, Ill.: Victor, 1974); Billie Hanks, Jr., and William A. Shell, eds., *Discipleship* (Grand Rapids: Zondervan, 1981); Francis M. Cosgrove, Jr., *Essentials of New Life* (Colorado Springs, Colo.: NavPress, 1978), and J. Dwight Pentecost, *Design for Discipleship* (Grand Rapids: Zondervan, 1971).

George Patterson has defined a church as "a fellowship of believers committed to obeying the Lord Jesus Christ."[19] Patterson insists that Christian commitment to Christ cannot be real unless built upon obedience to his basic commandments. Whatever the culture, the process illustrated by the discipling continuum of figure 23 should seek to commit the new converts to *obey* Christ in (1) faith and repentance, (2) baptism, (3) love, (4) the Lord's Supper, (5) prayer, (6) giving, and (7) witnessing.[20] The team should prepare inductive Bible studies for each of these subjects and require the new believers to work through them as part of the preparation for public confession of faith through water baptism.

Fig. 23

Continuum of Discipleship

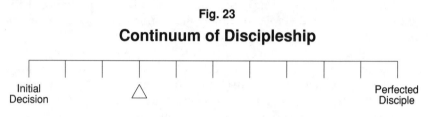

Vergil Gerber, *Discipling Through Theological Education by Extension*, 44.

Other factors play an important part in prebaptism instruction in many cultures. Church planters have found a need to give time to answering the multitude of questions generated in the minds of new converts by their introduction to the Scriptures and biblical doctrines. Many feel strongly that a new believer must not be baptized before the reality of conversion has been verified. Nevertheless, it must be admitted that baptisms reported in the New Testament came immediately upon or soon after conversion.[21] In spite of this, certain factors, such as the Roman Catholic belief concerning baptism, alert us to be cautious. It is certainly desirable that the true convert be obedient in baptism as soon as possible. Perhaps one of the underlying reasons for caution and delay among churches with a congregational form of government is that, once baptized, the adult new Christian becomes a voting member of the local church. This could conceivably pose a threat to the church's ministry should there be a sizeable number of new members who are not truly converted.

Activity 14 (Goal: event 12): Promote congregational activities that help unite all new believers in the target area (figure 24).

19. George A. Patterson, *Church Planting Through Obedience Oriented Teaching* (Pasadena, Calif.: William Carey Library, 1981), 1.
20. Gerber, *Discipling Through*, 44.
21. Patterson, *Church Planting*, 8–9.

Until formal organization of the new local church takes place, every effort should be made to foster congregational consciousness and

Fig. 24
Unite All New Converts

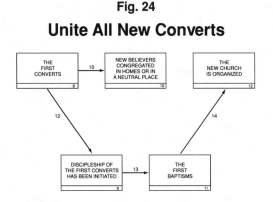

cohesion. It is to be recognized that certain evangelical groups or denominations do not consider formal organizational procedure to be important. Some do not count members as such. Therefore, denominational practice will vary widely at this point in the strategy.

Every new face is an encouragement to the nucleus as it is taking shape. Even at this early stage, loving, mutual caring and concern for one another reminiscent of the early days of the church in Jerusalem (Acts 2–5) should be facilitated. Planned social times together set the stage for fellowship and mutual sharing on a wider scale.

Initial Organization of the New Church

Activity 11 (Goal: event 12): Teach the new believers that which is basically prerequisite to membership in the local church and proceed to organize the new local church (figure 25).

Fig. 25
New Church Organized

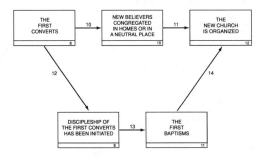

Every evangelical denomination or group has its own prerequisites or norms for membership in the local church. Therefore, the content of what must be taught to new believers as prospective members will vary considerably. The basic philosophy seems to be that no one should become a member of the local church unless he or she has been truly converted to Christ, has been baptized, and has a clear understanding of the nature of the church, the responsibilities of members, and is willing to abide by the doctrine and practice professed. One denomination in Portugal I know of, for example, requires that the nucleus wishing to be organized and recognized as a local church (1) have a suitable doctrinal statement, (2) invite other churches of like faith and order to meet to examine and approve those composing the nucleus, and (3) choose a pastor. Often an initial church constitution suggested by the church planting team is accepted during the phase of organization. Other factors that often determine the opportune time for the formal organization of a local church are (1) a certain number of baptized believers, (2) a certain level of financial capacity, (3) a permanent place to meet, and (4) elders competent to take responsibility.

Many church planters, such as Brock in the Philippines, who are evangelizing by means of Bible study groups in homes, feel that plans must be made for "a graduation from a Bible study group to a church . . . a move anticipated . . . from the beginning."[22] In Brock's experience, the birth of a new church happens within ten to fifteen weeks from the start of the home Bible study.

Initial Leadership

The need to develop local leaders should dictate the conduct of the life of the nucleus from the very beginning. Responsibilities must be shared *willingly* by the team members involved with the new believers. "There should be a large degree of self-government, self-support, and self-propagation at the time of birth."[23] This does not happen automatically! It entails serious determined awareness of what is happening to the attitudes of the believers as a result of each thing we do or implement in the growing nucleus. Brock, as an example, shares in detail how he does it in his field of service.[24]

The Team: What Now?

What happens to the church planting team as formal church organization begins to take shape? First, those team members who eventually intend to become members of the new church will join the growing

---

22. Brock, *Principles and Practice*, 88.
23. Ibid., 89.
24. Ibid., 63–93.

nucleus of baptized believers, giving their fellowship, counsel, and support. Second, the team should phase out its activity *as a team*, gradually transferring responsibilities and decision making to the growing nucleus. Third, local financial contributions in particular should be handled by the nucleus and *not* the team. Fourth, logically the team will be expected to suggest the first basic church organization and constitution. Fifth, those team members who decide not to become members of the new church will simply return to their own home church fellowship.

The organization of the new local church in our PERT plan (event 12) means that we have reached the *first major goal* in our church planting effort (see figure 6). Therefore, the "Pioneer Period" has terminated and the next PERT goals will have to do with the growth and organization of the new-born church.

PART 3

The Period of Growth and Organization

5

Social Concern and Evangelism

We are entering the phase in the process of planting the church that is extremely perplexing to a host of church planters, not to mention a large majority of established churches and their pastoral staffs. Hundreds of books have been published in recent years which zero-in on certain aspects of local church life and ministry. Many of the subjects in this spotlight are very biblical and sound doctrinally, but with all this popular attention they take on the appearance of fads. For instance, some today are talking of little but "worship." Others emphasize "spiritual gifts." Still others speak of "power encounter" as if it were a brand new concept. We worked alongside of some in Portugal who went to seed, so to speak, in what they called "freedom in the Spirit." These and similar ideas are valuable constituent elements for a live, growing church; yet for many there continues to be something lacking in practice.

What is lacking? Often the leaders have lost sight of (or never had) goals in line with Christ's evangelistic mandate. Many churches are turned in on themselves. They have forgotten God's goal for their existence. On the other hand, there are those leaders who want to reach out in evangelism, and even attempt to do so, but find church members disinterested.

Our long-range goal must constantly be kept up front—a mature church, capable and motivated to reproduce. Charles Brock notes that "if a church planter is fully aware of the need for 'thinking reproducible' in everything done, he will more likely plant a church capable of reproduction."[1] In this chapter we enter the third stage of our PERT strategy. The "baby" church must be nurtured and enabled to grow to maturity. If you will consult the PERT plan in figure 6 once again, you will note that there are nine parallel goals or events (15, 18, 21, 26, 30, 33, 35, 38, and 40). Those are nine ways in which the new church should begin to grow *simultaneously*. It is a matter of balance. In this book I am forced to discuss these nine goals one by one. In practice the church planter, and later the new church, are obliged to have all of them constantly in mind as they minister. We cannot afford to emphasize one or two to the detriment of others. Hosea was inspired to write, "Ephraim has become a cake not turned" (Hos. 7:8); in other words, half-baked! I fear that if he were alive today he could say the same about churches which are underdeveloped in one way or another. The main emphasis then is balance. Without doubt such equilibrium is absolutely necessary to achieve a spiritually healthy maturity, capable and motivated to reproduce.

In this chapter, therefore, I will consider Network II (see figure 6) which will develop the new church in the direction of a major goal in our plan—*a church that lives for others*. Two subjects are central to this goal: social concern and evangelism.

Social Concern

> *Activity 15 (Goal: event 13):* Try to make the acquaintance of more people of different levels of society. Become intimately familiar with the population of the target area (figure 26).

Fig. 26

Wider Contacts Initiated

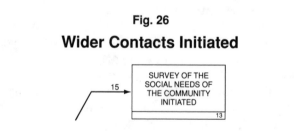

Our Lord and the apostles were very clear about the disciple's duty to others. Paul taught the Galatian churches that "as we have opportunity let us do good unto all men, especially unto them who are of the

1. Charles Brock, *The Principles and Practice of Indigenous Church Planting* (Nashville: Broadman, 1981), 55–61.

household of faith" (Gal. 6:10). A true believer in Christ will not hesi-
tate to do all in his power to help those in need. Jesus challenges us to
"let your light so shine before men, that they may see your good works,
and glorify your father which is in heaven" (Matt. 5:16). He gave further instruction in the parable of the good Samaritan (Luke 10:30–37).
In the law of love (Luke 10:27) we have an obvious mandate as
Christians to relieve suffering and to help those in need.[2]

Never before has our world been better informed by the international
news media. Oppression and exploitation of peoples in any part of the
globe is almost immediately known by the rest of the world population.
Political action on many fronts has alerted social consciousness to the
gross evils afflicting large sectors of the populations of many nations.
Human rights are constantly in focus, and rightly so. Evangelicals have
been caught up in a general demand for social "revolution," "change,"
"action," "concern"—"involvement." Due to this intense and growing
preoccupation within and without evangelical circles, it is to be
expected that widely differing opinions are being expressed. What is our
social responsibility before the underprivileged and oppressed peoples
of the world? The continuum in figure 27 shows a spectrum of view-
points as to the relationship between evangelism and social action as
expressed by a number of authors.[3] Evangelicals find themselves, in
general, grouped around areas 3-to-5 or 6-to-9 of this spectrum.[4]

I find myself in the first group, affirming the primacy of evangelism.
Roland Allen's testimony, in speaking of his experience as a missionary
in Africa, is a healthy warning as to how well-meaning evangelism can
be entrapped by an undue emphasis on social action:

> In the beginning we put Christ first. Belief in Christ was the one thing
> needful. . . . Conversion to Christ was the first thing, the only thing that
> really mattered, and our attention must be given first and before all else
> to leading men to Christ. But more and more as we developed these
> social activities they became first in time, and two serious consequences
> followed: (1) . . . we tended to accept the position that reform of condi-
> tions was a necessary antecedent to the living of a Christian life. . . .
> (2) social advance must be based on some other foundation than faith in
> Christ.[5]

2. Adapted from Melvin L. Hodges, *A Guide to Church Planting* (Chicago: Moody, 1973), 85.

3. C. Peter Wagner, John Yoder, John Stott, Ron Sider, Orlando Costas, Arthur P. Johnston, Vinay Samuel, Chris Sugden, and Donald A. McGavran.

4. Arthur P. Johnston, "A Summary and Evaluation of CRESER—Consultation on the Relationship Between Evangelism and Social Responsibility" (Deerfield, Ill.: photo-copied, typed ms., 1982), 6.

5. Roland Allen, *The Spontaneous Expansion of the Church and the Causes Which Hinder It* (Grand Rapids: Eerdmans, 1962), 81–83.

Fig. 27

Evangelism/Social Action Continuum

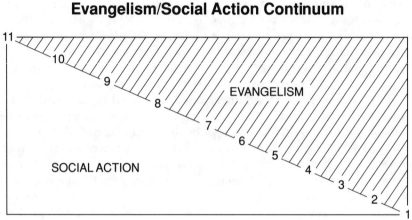

1. Social action is a *betrayal* of evangelism.

2. Social action is a *distraction* from evangelism.

3. Social action is a *means* to evangelism.

4. Social action is a *manifestation* of evangelism.

5. Social action is a *result* or *consequence* of evangelism.

6. Social action is a *partner* of evangelism.

7. Social action and evangelism are equally important but genuinely *distinct* aspects of the total mission of the church.

8. Social action is *part of* the good news—evangelism.

9. Social action *is* evangelism.

10. Social action should take *priority* over evangelism.

11. Evangelism is politics because *salvation is social justice.*

Adapted from Arthur P. Johnston, "A Summary and Evaluation of CRESER—Consultation on the Relationship Between Evangelism and Social Responsibility" (Deerfield, Ill.: photocopied, typed ms, 1982), 6.

I take the position in this chapter that social concern is sometimes a *means*, sometimes a *bridge of love*, and at other times a *result* or *consequence* of evangelism. In our PERT plan evangelism and social concern are simultaneous. Although the evangelistic mandate concerns the eternal souls of men, the local church encounters them in their physical surroundings and out of necessity must deal with their needs on an earthly plane insofar as means permit.

Activity 15 has to do with *contact*, contact that goes beyond the initial demographic penetration before the church was planted. In many countries the evangelicals are less than 1 percent of the population. This can only mean that they are overwhelmingly unknown to the average citizen. No wonder the general populace confuses the evangelicals with more active sects, such as the Mormons and Jehovah's Witnesses! The sects and cults are simply *making contact* with large numbers of people. By and large the evangelicals are not.

How can our new church make contact with the people on different levels in the target area effectively? Attention must be given to *social structure*. David J. Hesselgrave regards social structure as referring to "those social relations which seem to be of critical importance for the behavior of members of the society."[6] Donald McGavran uses the term "homogeneous units" to describe any significant groupings in a society. He claims that people "do not join churches where services are conducted in a language they do not understand, or where members have noticeable higher degree of education, wear better clothes, and are obviously of a different sort."[7] McGavran adds: "New Christians must fight both to be really Christian *and* to maintain *unbroken contact* with their kin. . . . They must be both solid with and separate from their people."[8]

It would seem to be sound reasoning that we best penetrate the community through our first converts. They should be strongly encouraged to remain in contact with their families and kin—to shine in their darkness. Converts are natural contacts with society at any and all levels. Through them other opportunities for contact will come.

Any legitimate and practical means to increase the awareness of the community to the presence of an evangelical church should be used. Contacts can be made with other churches, school officials, government leaders, business leaders, and professionals who provide services in the community. Church planter Brock cautions us, however, to be careful of what we consider to be legitimate means. He feels that, if we are to lead the new church in "thinking reproducible," we must not employ any means—material things, strategy, and kinds of leadership—which the national local congregation does not have at its disposal. Otherwise, we are clearly working against our long-range goal.[9]

Activity 16 (Goal: event 14): Observe the social conditions and felt needs of the target community (figure 28).

6. David J. Hesselgrave, *Planting Churches Cross-Culturally: A Guide for Home and Foreign Missions* (Grand Rapids: Baker, 1980), 162–63.
7. Donald A. McGavran, *Understanding Church Growth* (Grand Rapids: Eerdmans, 1970), 306.
8. Ibid., 307.
9. Brock, *Principles and Practice*, 56–61.

Fig. 28
Community Needs Understood

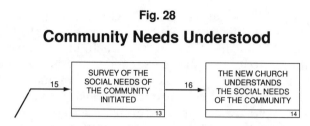

If a church is to live for others, it must seek to know who the "others" are and to understand their needs. That is why F. Jack Redford advocates that a new church *cultivate* the community by identifying its needs and its interests.[10] Problems may be opportunities for valuable evangelistic contact. Even though our mandate is to evangelize, we also have a command to love and to show compassion. "Bridges of love" to unsaved hearts often consist of actions that meet people's felt needs.

One church planter in a new work saw the large number of people who were moving into new apartments in the area. Gifted members of the fledgling church took their power tools and offered their expertise to install cabinets and fixtures, drill holes, repair furniture and render other valuable assistance free of charge. This proved an excellent way to meet obvious felt needs of the hour. A pastor in São Paulo, Brazil, told me of a Christian woman in a high-rise building who decided to contact people in her building by spending time each day riding the elevators. When she would observe a mother struggling with small children and a load of groceries and other purchases getting into the elevator, she would offer her help and accompany the woman to her apartment. This generated a warm response and an invitation to come in for a cup of coffee. Precious contact was made in ideal circumstances, along with an opportunity to answer the question, "Why are you doing this?" Other community needs might include transportation to the doctor, moving belongings to new quarters, supplying necessary household items, food, and many other real needs. In our work in Portugal we encountered such problems as the need for child-care, alcoholism, lonely senior citizens, single-parent families, drug abuse, and the highest illiteracy in western Europe. Every target community will be unique in a sense. The local church must demonstrate, in Jesus' name, the sensitivity the Lord Jesus showed when he noticed that the multitude following him had no food (Matt. 15:32).

Activity 17 (Goal: event 15): Make a plan that will mobilize the church to help meet social needs within its possibilities (figure 29).

10. F. Jack Redford, *Planting New Churches* (Nashville: Broadman, 1978), 54.

Fig. 29
Social Program Moving

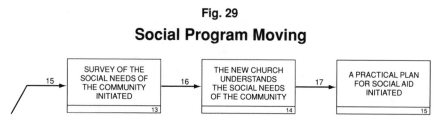

Each local church must act within its physical capabilities as needs are identified in the community. It should be obvious that the average congregation in any part of the world has limitations as to how much and in what ways it can reasonably direct help to relieve the felt social needs of people surrounding it. If Christian social concern truly consists of acting in God's love, it exists not only to meet felt needs, but primarily to melt and prepare hearts for Gospel witness. The core of the impetus for what is done socially should be to provide a *means* through which God's love is communicated. Child day-care centers, classes to teach people to read, free nursing service, the dispensing of medicines, and the recuperation of drug addicts are examples of social help being offered by local evangelical churches around the world. Churches have been involved in giving relief and shelter to earthquake victims. In areas of drought and famine some international evangelical relief agencies prefer to work through local churches. There is no lack of practical opportunities. Local churches should use these opportunities as "bridges of God's love" to reach out to those who are not only in dire need physically and morally, but whose souls are lost eternally without Christ!

Aggressive Evangelism

We now turn to the parallel and simultaneous chain of events aimed at establishing an aggressive program of evangelism. McGavran asserts that the church will achieve living contacts of involvement with the surrounding community as it undertakes "continuous and costly and Spirit-directed finding of the lost."[11] This is the most important way to live for others because it has eternal significance.

Activity 18 (Goal: event 16): Give training in personal evangelism to church members (figure 30).

Mobilization and Motivation

Every member of the church—in fact, *every believer*—ought to know how to share his or her faith. If Christians are to penetrate the commu-

11. McGavran, *Understanding Church Growth*, 309.

Fig. 30
Church Ready for Evangelism

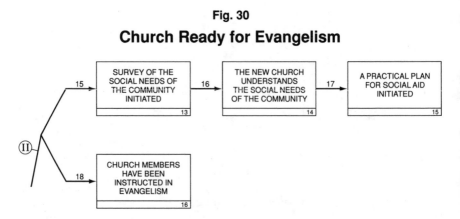

nity with their witness they must know *how* to share Christ with others. Church growth leaders Charles L. Chaney and Ron S. Lewis write that biblically and historically "it has been *the laity mobilized and motivated* to spiritual ministry that has produced the spontaneous expansion of the Church."[12] It should be our goal as church planters that every person in the church be able to do effective personal evangelism whenever and wherever possible.

Of course this will only be achieved as each individual is spiritually *motivated*. How then can the laity of a local church be both mobilized and motivated? Six sound church growth principles are suggested by Chaney and Lewis. First, Bible-study is a top priority; second, leaders are growing in maturity; third, there is a growth atmosphere; fourth, small cell groups function; fifth, members are open to honest self-appraisal or evaluation, and sixth, there are new units or people, whether converts or transfers from elsewhere.[13]

At this point I must emphasize again the need to synchronize the development of these facets with the remainder of our PERT plan, especially with everything in Network III (see figure 6). As the church grows it will become evident that the church cannot proceed in effective evangelism and discipleship (including follow-up) until it is *spiritually* strong as a congregation. The plan, diagrammed in figure 6, must be constantly kept in mind in order to achieve the balance necessary.

Personal Evangelism Instruction

Techniques in personal evangelism are taught through a variety of types of materials. The leaders of the local church should study these

12. Charles L. Chaney and Ron S. Lewis, *Design for Church Growth* (Nashville: Broadman, 1977), 149. Emphasis author's.
13. Ibid., 45–63.

materials, especially those that teach *how* to witness. Methods must be adapted by those evangelizing to be effective in the local culture and religious situation.

One system which has been well received by evangelicals is Campus Crusade's seminar of about fifteen hours of instruction in how to witness using the *Four Spiritual Laws* booklet. Instruction is accompanied by challenging messages on living the Spirit-filled life. Many local churches relate benefits from these seminars.

Bible institutes and seminaries offer TEE courses in personal evangelism. These extension courses usually last several weeks, using programed texts and/or cassettes.

D. James Kennedy's "Evangelism Explosion" program is proving a very successful tool in local churches and includes beginning and advanced levels.

Kennedy's personal frustration as a young minister is typical of many who are unprepared to witness to the lost. A church intending to reproduce itself must overcome this obstacle by instructing its members in evangelism. Pastors and church leaders who are personal evangelists can and should lead their congregations. It is thrilling to see the joy of a once inactive Christian when someone else is led to faith in Christ through their personal witness! I have seen this happen many times. It does not take too many of these lay evangelists in a local church to literally "set it on fire" for the Lord.

Activity 19 (Goal: event 17): Study and experiment how best to evangelize in the target area (figure 31).

Fig. 31

Evangelistic Methods Chosen

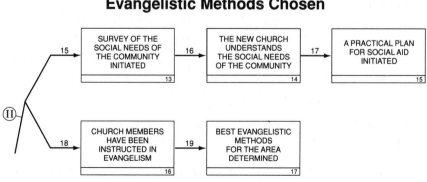

In my discussion of the pioneer period of planting the church, some decisions were made *before* the initial evangelism took place in the target area (see activity 6, p. 57). Now that the church is underway, ideas which proved successful should be continued and amplified to involve more participants. Moreover, since a new church has been organized with converts from the area, much more can be attempted now in aggressive evangelistic penetration. More than one evangelistic method should be used. As we plan and act, we should keep the Great Commission of Matthew 28:19 fresh in our memory and vision. Remember that:

1. *All* the people in the area are important to God.
2. *All* are our target population.
3. *Any* method used must enable us to contact these people.
4. Once contacted, each must come to really "hear" the gospel if they are to repent and believe (Mark 1:15).
5. The church must *want* to make contacts.
6. Christ's love and compassion must fill church members' hearts.
7. The biblical ideal is that the *whole* membership become involved in personal witness.

Among the valid methods we used to make evangelistic contacts in our work were door to door surveys, telephone surveys, extended-family relationships, acquaintance surveys (social contacts), film projections in public places, social assistance contacts, distribution of literature with the church address, and neighborhood Bible-study cells.

Neighborhood Bible studies proved to be a great blessing. Howard A. Snyder offers lavish praise for the potential of cell groups to revive the modern church:

A small group of eight to twelve people meeting together informally in homes is the *most effective structure* for the communication of the gospel in modern secular urban society. Such groups are better suited to the mission of the church in today's urban world than are traditional church services, institutional church programs or the mass communication media. Methodologically speaking, the small group offers the best hope for the discovery and use of spiritual gifts and for renewal within the church. . . . The small group was the basic unit of the church's life during its first two centuries. [14]

Brock, Ralph Neighbour, and others do rightly alert us to the danger of allowing Bible-study cells to become smug retreats where Christians

14. Howard A. Snyder, *The Problem of Wine Skins: Church Structure in a Technological Age* (Downers Grove, Ill.: Inter-Varsity, 1975), 139. Snyder presents an excellent chapter on small groups.

Fig. 32

Productive Prospect Search Form

On this form list your own acquaintances in the various categories.
Use it when interviewing acquaintances or contacts.

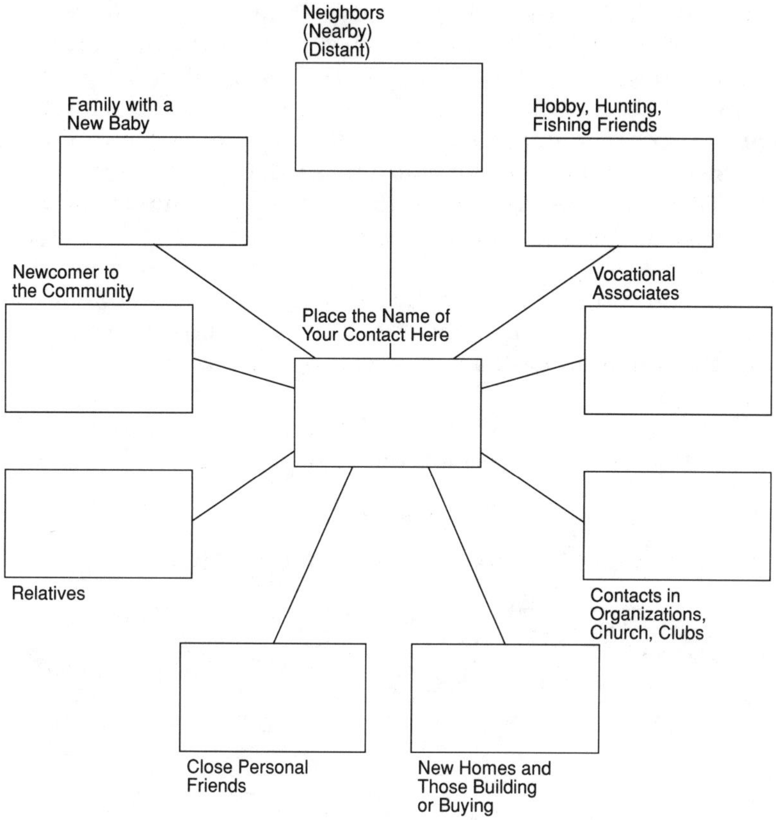

Neighbors
(Nearby)
(Distant)

Family with a
New Baby

Hobby, Hunting,
Fishing Friends

Newcomer to
the Community

Vocational
Associates

Place the Name of
Your Contact Here

Relatives

Contacts in
Organizations,
Church, Clubs

Close Personal
Friends

New Homes and
Those Building
or Buying

Adapted from Charles L. Chaney and Ron S. Lewis,
Design For Church Growth (Nashville: Broadman, 1977), 216.

soak up more and more Bible knowledge and fellowship, thus losing their vision for reaching a lost world. They should rather be constantly sharpened up as evangelism outposts!

A noteworthy scheme elaborated by the late Pastor Ken Stephens[15] of Arizona has been successfully used cross-culturally. Called *Discipleship Evangelism*, it consists of four lessons normally administered to a couple in their home over four or five weeks. Lesson titles are (1) "The Bible—Its Origin," (2) "The Bible—Its Theme," (3) "The

15. Ken Stephens, *Discipleship Evangelism* (Scottsdale, Ariz.: Good Life, 1978).

Bible—Its Person," and (4) "The Bible—Its Relevance." Initial contacts made during systematic door-to-door surveys determine who might be interested in a study of the Bible. Definite appointments are then made with those interested—not more than one session a week. The invitation to decision is not made until the person can reasonably understand the fundamentals underlying decision (as noted in discussion of activity 8, pp. 65–67). Also, this plan envisions the evangelizing of both husband and wife together. Copies of the lesson outlines are left with the couple for review and scrutiny after each session. An attempt is made to encourage questions. I evangelized one couple in Portugal who insisted on tape recording our times together over the entire five weeks. They then used these as training tapes for themselves and have since been the instruments for winning a large number of other acquaintances.

Figure 32 reproduces a very interesting tool suggested by Chaney and Lewis for discovering evangelistic prospects through a single contact. It can be culturally adapted to a local situation.[16]

Activity 20 (Goal: event 18): Elaborate and execute plans for concrete steps to evangelize the target community (figure 33).

Fig. 33
Aggressive Evangelism in Motion

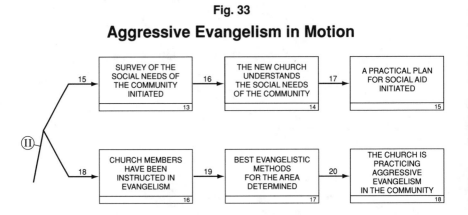

The Holy Spirit must be recognized as the "general" at all times (Acts 1:8). A prayerful spirit of discipleship in all strategy, planning, and management will insure effective evangelism. Without the Spirit in the leading role the church has no convicting power (John 16:7–11).

This fact does not negate the need for adequate human administration (see chapter 8). PERT principles explained in chapter 2 can be applied to any planning operation, including those that concern evan-

16. Chaney and Lewis, *Design*, 216.

gelism. Specific evangelistic goals or objectives must be identified and the corresponding activities determined for reaching each goal. Evangelistic planning of this sort must become a routine characteristic of the church if it is to experience growth and obey Christ's Commission in Matthew 28:19. People must be matched with specific methods to be used and jobs to be accomplished. They must be supplied with literature, personal evangelism materials, maps, and specific directions that avoid confusion. Those gifted by the Holy Spirit for administration and who show organizational skills will be especially valuable in strategic planning and execution.

By achieving the goals of Network II (events 15 and 18), we have reached the *second major goal* in our church planting effort (see figure 6): *We have a church that exists or lives for others* (event 41). This is a fundamental characteristic of any church capable of reproducing itself. C. Peter Wagner comments that a mature church

> is successfully discipling the non-Christians in its own community. Growth comes from conversions from the world as well as from biological and transfer growth. Not only does it grow as a congregation, but the mature church sends forth people to plant daughter churches in neighboring communities. Finally, it has developed a cross-cultural vision for planting churches in other cultures, whether near or far . . . one of the most advanced signs of maturity.[17]

The Spirit probably will call some members of the church to become his servants elsewhere. This will be a natural opportunity for the church to eventually participate in the cost of their further preparation and ministry at home or abroad. World missions is at the heart of local church evangelism, as is seen clearly in Acts 1:8—the witness that started in Jerusalem and is yet being carried "to the remotest part of the earth."

17. C. Peter Wagner, *Frontiers in Missionary Strategy* (Chicago: Moody, 1971), 166–67.

6

Spiritual Life

With this chapter we begin to think through a group of activities our PERT plan calls *Network III*. These activities are concerned with *the inner workings of the life of the church* as it grows to maturity and beyond. You will recall from chapter 2 that this network consists of five subnetworks. Each of these focuses a specific topic of basic importance to the very life of the local church. The five topics are *liturgy, administration, spiritual life, finances* and *self-image*, or *identity*.

How should we *plan* for the church to *grow* in these five areas of her life? Once again consult the complete PERT chart, as well as the small, reduced chart in figure 6. Note that these five objectives are integral parts of one of our major church planting goals: *a church that takes care of itself*. Such a church is well on its way to maturity. The activities to be studied here suggest how to reach this major goal.

It is important to remind ourselves that the development of each of these subnetworks should be carried on along with or parallel to the development of Network II (see chapter 5) and Network IV (see chapter 11). Our preoccupation should be *balanced growth* in the areas covered by networks II, III, and IV. A careful analysis of why many existing churches throughout the world are not reproducing will underscore the need for balance in growth and organization.

In graphically designing the PERT plan, I have purposely placed the spiritual life of the local church at the center or the very core of Network III. If a church does not give due attention to achieving the goals in this chain, it will eventually become a rather formalistic and "cool" group of people with little if any mutual love. Certainly, it will lack a passion for the lost. The situation in the Corinthian church led the apostle Paul to call them "carnal" Christians (1 Cor. 3:1–3). Their lack of spirituality led to abuses in public worship, in their exercise of their spiritual gifts, in church administration, in finances, and in self-image. Under the circumstances their testimony to Jesus was greatly impaired. As such they were called "babes in Christ"; they could not be treated as adults. Reproduction was improbable; babies don't reproduce. The church disarmed itself spiritually!

The Teaching of Stewardship

> *Activity 30 (Goal: event 27):* Carefully teach the scriptural doctrine of stewardship (figure 34).

Fig. 34
Consciousness of Stewardship Responsibilities

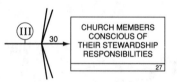

There is a reticence among many national and missionary church planters to bring up the subject of money. This is especially true in cultures with a Roman Catholic background. The Roman Catholic church has a notoriously bad reputation in many areas when it comes to money. Portuguese evangelicals, for example, many of whom have a background in Romanism, tend to be slow to mention money for fear of alienating new people.

The Deformity of Emphasis

Contrary to the common understanding of the average Christian, the New Testament doctrine of *stewardship* goes far beyond finances to all that a Christian possesses—time and talent as well as money. Stewardship has to do with the Christian's very life. David J. Hesselgrave is absolutely correct in reflecting that "missionary-evangelists do not give enough attention to basic biblical and psychological principles as they relate to stewardship."[1] I am absolutely convinced

---

1. David J. Hesselgrave, *Planting Churches Cross-Culturally: A Guide for Home and Foreign Missions* (Grand Rapids: Baker, 1980), 340.

that this doctrine has been *deformed* and *disfigured* in the minds of most of our church members by an undue primary emphasis on money and finances.

For the new believer in our church planting process, there really is nothing more important than his or her obedience to a biblical understanding of what it means to be a *Christian* steward. This simply means that it constitutes one of the high priorities in the discipleship process. Those in leadership in the new church must tactfully, yet boldly, explore this subject with each new convert until they are satisfied that what God says is understood and can be acted upon. This is vital to Christian living.

The Definition of a Steward

Fundamental to an understanding of stewardship is the meaning of *steward* in God's Word. Essentially, a steward is someone who administers, manages, or dispenses something that belongs to someone else.[2] To the Corinthians Paul wrote, "Do you not know that your body is a temple of the Holy Spirit who is in you, whom you have from God, and that you are not your own? For you have been bought with a price: Therefore glorify God in your body" (1 Cor. 6:19–20). This means that in the Christian context, the new-born convert literally belongs to God. He technically doesn't own a thing, including his own person! He is commanded to honor God with his body. A Christian, then, has become a steward—God's steward. Everything he *is* and apparently possesses has been confided to him to wisely administer for the Master (as in the parable of the talents, Matt. 25:14–30).

I have included in figure 35 two lists of basic stewardship principles, one from Paul Lindholm[3] and the other from Ralph Martin.[4] Paul Lindholm, in his excellent little booklet, *Principles and Practice of*

2. New Testament vocabulary. Three words appear in the Greek concordance and lexicon to express (1) to be a steward, (2) stewardship itself, and (3) the steward. In Luke 16:2, the parable of the wise steward, οἰκονομέω was to *manage* something that was not his. In Luke 16:2–4, the same parable, the focus is on οἰκονομία or *management* as the steward's job. Paul speaks of this as an apostolic office in 1 Corinthians 9:17; Ephesians 3:2, and Colossians 1:25. Trust, commission, and administration of the gospel, the Word, and the grace of God are involved in Paul's apostolic stewardship. In Luke 12:42, and 16:1, 3, and 8; 1 Corinthians 4:2, and Galatians 4:2 the steward is spoken of as a private manager of someone else's property, οἰκονόμος. In this sense, Romans 16:23 speaks of Erastus, who served as city treasurer, as, literally, the steward of the city, indicating his care for public funds and property. First Corinthians 4:1; Titus 1:7, and 1 Peter 4:10 speak of Christians as such stewards and administrators of spiritual or divine things (the mysteries of God, God's work, God's grace).

3. Paul R. Lindholm, *Principles and Practice of Christian Stewardship* (Madras, India: Christian Literature Society, 1965), 4–13.

4. Ralph P. Martin, *Worship in the Early Church*, rev. ed. (Grand Rapids: Eerdmans, 1975), 84–85; cited in Hesselgrave, *Planting Churches*, 337.

Fig. 35

Stewardship Principles

Seven Basic Principles of Christian Stewardship

Principles	Scripture
1. God is sovereign.	Deut. 4:39; 1 Chron. 29:11; Eph. 4:6
2. Man is to be God's servant.	Gen. 2:15; Isa. 44:21; Luke 17:10; 1 Cor. 3:5; 1 Pet. 2:16
3. God is Creator, Sustainer and Owner of all.	Acts 4:24; 1 Cor. 10:26; Col. 1:17
4. God has entrusted us with his grace.	Matt. 25:27; Luke 12:42; 1 Cor. 4:1; 1 Pet. 4:10
5. Man is accountable to God for his stewardship.	Matt. 16:27; 25:19; Luke 12:48; Rom. 14:10; 14:12
6. God's mercy, grace, and love should motivate us.	Rom. 12:1; 2 Cor. 8:9; 1 John 4:19
7. The purpose: that God may be glorified.	1 Cor. 10:31; Eph. 1:12; 1 Pet. 4:11

Adapted from Paul R. Lindholm, *Principles and Practice of Christian Stewardship* (Madras, India: Christian Literature Society, 1965), 4–13.

Seven Basic Stewardship Principles from 2 Corinthians 8 and 9

1. The basis of stewardship is that God has given bountifully to his people.
2. The most important offering is the commitment of one's own life to God.
3. All Christian giving is prompted by divine grace, yet is voluntary, eager, and cheerful.
4. Stewardship is to be offered in accordance with one's ability and the needs of others.
5. God is no man's debtor.
6. Churches and their people should be fair and open in their financial dealings.
7. Concern for the welfare of others creates a bond of love between giver and recipient and calls forth the praise of God.

Ralph P. Martin, *Worship in the Early Church* (Grand Rapids: Eerdmans, 1975), 84–85, cited by David J. Hesselgrave, *Planting Churches Cross-Culturally* (Grand Rapids: Baker Book House, 1980), 337.

Christian Stewardship, also suggests seven stewardship responsibilities with Bible references for inductive study.[5]

Stewardship Strategy

These principles and resulting responsibilities should be patiently taught to all new Christians. We have found that those who are diligently taught from the Scriptures become good stewards of what the Lord has committed to their charge. The idea that we are managing what does not belong to us is certainly common in daily secular life. Employees in business are stewards of the property of the company assigned to them. This could be a company car, a tool from the tool-crib in a factory, the book checked out from a library, or even the baby left in the care of a baby-sitter. Each person is a steward of something that is not his or hers. New Christians must be led to see this.

In my church planting ministry I have emphasized six principles with good results: (1) Believers *completely* belong to the Lord. (2) Each one is, therefore, a steward. (3) A "temple" (physical body) has been confided to the care of each one: for this reason one does not have the right to abuse or poison his body. (4) Each one has received three basic "gifts" to administer or manage for God (the rightful owner)—material possessions, natural talents, and spiritual gifts. (5) The Lord expects his stewards to be spiritual, dedicated, joyful, wise, and generous in their administration. (6) God will one day require an accounting from each Christian of that person's stewardship.

Finances

The above biblical concepts lay a foundation for enthusiastic *financial* stewardship. I have found that people are motivated to be obedient in matters of money once they have acquired an understanding of the whole stewardship picture from Scripture. Charles Brock and others engaged in serious church planting concur that, to the extent possible, the local body of believers should be encouraged and allowed to shoulder the responsibility for the expenses incurred in every aspect of church life from its very beginning. Details as to what is involved will be dis-

---

5. Lindholm, *Principles and Practice*, 16–29. Lindholm's list of stewardship responsibilities includes: (1) Reconcile others to God as an ambassador for Christ: 2 Kings 7:1–9; 1 Corinthians 4:1; 2 Corinthians 5:19–20; 1 Thessalonians 2:4, and 1 Peter 2:9. (2) Make the most of one's time: Psalms 118:24; Proverbs 18:9; John 9:4, and Ephesians 5:14–17. (3) Use one's body for God: Luke 6:46; 10:29–36, and 37; John 3:36 and 15:10; Romans 12:1, and 1 Corinthians 6:19–20. (4) Use all material possessions for God; they belong to him: Leviticus 25:23; Deuteronomy 10:14; Haggai 2:8, and 1 Corinthians 10:26. (5) Use one's home to worship God: Acts 2:46–47; 12:12; 16:13–15, 40, and 18:1–4; Romans 16:3–6, and Colossians 4:15. (6) Be familiar with God's Word: Psalms 119:72, 103–5; Matthew 4:4; Acts 20:32, and 2 Timothy 3:16–17. (7) Pray always for our brethren: Matthew 9:36–38; Luke 6:28, and 18:1; Acts 7:57–8:1, and Ephesians 6:18.

cussed in the PERT subnetwork concerning finances (chapter 9). Unless the small group or house church strategy is normally followed, urban church planting, in particular, faces an enormous obstacle: the need for a meeting place. City rents are prohibitive for the newborn church. The temptation is to provide this from an outside source, such as a mother church, association of churches, or missionary society. Missiologists and urban strategists today are seriously challenging this practice.

The Discovery and Nurture of Spiritual Gifts

Activity 31 (Goal: event 28): Teach clearly the biblical doctrine concerning spiritual gifts, encouraging each believer to discover his or her gift or gifts (figure 36).

Fig. 36
Spiritual Gifts in Evidence

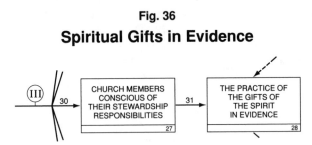

Volumes have been written by evangelicals in recent years about the gifts of the Holy Spirit. The charismatic controversy has spurred in-depth study by a number of well-known Bible scholars who, depending upon their theological roots, sometimes reach discordant conclusions. One such author, a seminary colleague, Leslie B. Flynn, writes:

> Paul taught about gifts from the very beginning of every new church. He wished each assembly to develop spiritually in normal and unde-layed fashion. New churches with all new believers had no members adequately mature to qualify as elders or deacons. But thrown upon the power of the Holy Spirit to put into practice Paul's teaching on the dis-cernment and discovery of spiritual gifts, some members grew suffi-ciently to be chosen as elders on Paul's return visit not long later (Acts 14:21–23). Through the exercise of gifts, saints had been edified.[6]

"In a very real sense, every member of the church is a 'person gift' to all the others," adds Hesselgrave.[7] A living body is a warm interrelated

---

6. Leslie B. Flynn, *Nineteen Gifts of the Holy Spirit: Which Do You Have?* (Wheaton, Ill.: Victor, 1974), 10.

7. Hesselgrave, *Planting Churches*, 109.

organism. Believers in a local church enjoy a distinct privilege of building up one another (Eph. 4:16). It also is a responsibility. This is why the leaders of the church should actively help *each* member to identify gifts and, once identified, to find where his or her gifts fit into the total life and ministry of the body (1 Pet. 4:10).

Baptism of the Holy Spirit and Gifts

Undergirding the fact that *every* Christian has been spiritually gifted for service in and through the "body" is the abiding presence of the Holy Spirit who personally indwells every true believer in Jesus Christ (Rom. 8:9). It is this initial baptism of the Spirit (1 Cor. 12:13), according to the apostle Paul, that equips each new Christian for active service to others (1 Cor. 12:7; Eph. 4:7, and 1 Pet. 4:10).[8] This basic doctrine must be taught and acted upon if the church is to achieve the goal of PERT event 42, a church that takes care of itself. All the members are thus capacitated by the Spirit to jointly participate in the edification of the church as a body. No one should be allowed to have an inferiority complex. According to the apostle Peter, this is one way in which all Christians can become "good stewards of the manifold grace of God" (1 Pet. 4:10). God dispenses *his* grace by means of *his* stewards—common believers related to one another in *his* church.

The Gifts and Their Discovery

As intimated above, a spiritual gift is a Spirit-given ability for Christian service. It must never be confused with a natural talent (or native ability), which we must admit is also God-given. Flynn writes that "our natural facilities may well point the direction in which our gifts will be used."[9] Likewise, we must be careful not to confuse gifts with offices (apostle, prophet, evangelist, pastor, teacher), with ministries (such as Paul's to the Gentiles), with fruit (as in Gal. 5:22–23), or with spirituality (1 Corinthians 7). Flynn counts eighteen gifts in Paul's writings (Rom. 12:3–8; 1 Cor. 12:8–10 and 28–30, and Eph. 4:11). There may be others not listed in Scripture.

How can the church leaders encourage believers to *discover* their spiritual gifts? First of all, encourage them to get involved in Christian service of various kinds. Certain spiritual abilities will surface. Then, teach them to be attentive to their desires and inclinations. Experience shows that there is a relationship between desire, a gift, and God's call to use it. Also, encourage them to dedicate themselves to the gift or

---

8. For a systematic study of this subject see John R. W. Stott, *The Baptism and Fullness of the Holy Spirit* (Downers Grove, Ill.: Inter-Varsity, 1974), and Merrill F. Unger, *The Baptism and Gifts of the Holy Spirit* (Chicago: Moody, 1974).

9. Flynn, *Nineteen Gifts*, 23.

gifts that they are attracted to. It is a step of commitment. Leaders must also help them to develop the gift by faithful use of it. Gifts must be exercised (1 Tim. 4:14–15 and 2 Tim. 4:5). Beyond this, observe if they delight in using their gift. In the Greek, *gift* (*"charisma"*) is related to *joy* (*"chara"*). Personal satisfaction is involved. There is another subtle factor: the discernment of fellow-believers. A believer's spiritual gifts are usually recognized by the brethren (Acts 6:3 and 16:1–3).[10]

Gifts of Leadership

Spiritual leaders are not made by election or appointment, by men or any combination of men, nor by conferences or synods. Only God can make them. Simply holding a position of importance does not constitute one a leader. Nor does taking courses in leadership or resolving to become a leader. The only method is that of *qualifying* to be a leader. . . . Spiritual leadership is a thing of the Spirit and is conferred by God alone.[11]

J. Oswald Sanders here sets out a most important preoccupation of church planters and of newly planted congregations—leadership. It is certainly true that no organization is stronger than its leadership. Raising up spiritual leadership should be a concern as we pray, think, plan, and work in the local church. It is of top priority, not only at the time the team is thinking of organizing the baby church (see PERT event 12), but also as the church grows. As the new Christians assume their stewardship responsibilities and as they begin to exercise their spiritual gifts, they must be taught how to recognize and select those gifted and spiritually qualified for leadership.[12]

Everyone exercising leadership in the local church should have this gift of the Spirit. In examining the Greek vocabulary for *leader* or *leadership* in Romans 12:8 (προΐστημι), 1 Corinthians 12:28 (κυβερνήσις), and Hebrews 13:7, 17, 24 (ἡγέομαι), we find that this gift enables a leader to superintend, preside, govern, administer, command, and rule or lead. The possession of this gift gives a person an overwhelming sense of mission—an inner spiritual drive toward his goals. Sanders gives a clue as to how we might be helped in identifying those with spiritual leadership. Real leadership qualities, he observes, "are to be found in those who are willing to suffer for the sake of objectives great enough to demand their wholehearted obedience."[13]

Two secular authors, Warren Bennis and Burt Nanus, in their recent

10. Ibid., 192–204.
11. J. Oswald Sanders, *Spiritual Leadership* (Chicago: Moody, 1967), 17.
12. Hesselgrave, *Planting Churches*, 349.
13. Sanders, *Spiritual Leadership*, 17.

book, *Leaders: The Strategies for Taking Charge*,[14] list four basic strategies employed by effective leaders:

1. Good leaders are persons with a focused vision that attracts the attention and the commitment of others.
2. Effective leaders position themselves within the tradition, history, and social patterns of the group in which they are functioning.
3. Effective leaders communicate their vision meaningfully.
4. Good leaders deploy themselves so as to empower others.[15]

As is true with other spiritual gifts, leadership can only be exercised effectively when the person is filled with the Spirit. Such a leader will then demonstrate the qualities Paul mentioned to his fellow team members, Timothy and Titus (1 Tim. 3:1–13 and Titus 1:7–9), as well as the fruit of the Spirit expected of the whole church (Gal. 5:22–23). A leader who is Spirit-filled will exhibit discipline, vision, wisdom, clear decision, courage, humility, clean humor, righteous anger or wrath, patience, friendship, tact and diplomacy, and executive ability.[16] Because it is of the Spirit, spiritual leadership is subject to the continual perfecting work of the Spirit.

Each evangelical group or denomination has its own leadership structure, job descriptions, and titles, but the tasks are mostly the same. There are superintending roles. There are pastoral roles. There are serving roles. The New Testament reveals an emerging administration at the local level, which was increasingly needed as the churches multiplied and grew in numbers (Acts 6:1–6). The first elders were appointed by the apostles themselves, who were the church planters (Titus 1:5). Local churches which came into being without the presence of an apostle would have had to use some other procedure to recognize their leaders. We know from the New Testament records that before calling leaders, the apostles and the church spent time in prayer and fasting. Whether or not we should proceed exactly as they did depends largely upon the local situation and our tradition. David W. Shenk and Ervin R. Stutzman are right, however, when they say that leadership selection is "a spiritual exercise in which the voice of the Holy Spirit must be heard, or we labor in vain."[17] Our purpose in this book is to focus our attention on the *biblical qualifications* all leaders should possess. Those listed by Paul in 1 Timothy and Titus are explicit. The local body of

14. New York: Harper and Row, 1986.
15. David W. Shenk and Ervin R. Stutzman, *Creating Communities of the Kingdom* (Scottdale, Pa.: Herald, 1988), 163.
16. Sanders, *Spiritual Leadership*, 43–69.
17. Shenk and Stutzman, *Creating Communities*, 169–70.

believers should be made aware of what *God* expects of their leaders as revealed in his Word. Titles and structure should then be designed and staffed with utmost care to choose a few leaders whose gifts are recognized. Hesselgrave warns that, "if leadership is not shared, it runs the risk of being dictatorial and occasioning division. If it is shared too widely, it runs the risk of being unwieldy and ineffective."[18]

The gift of spiritual leadership, then, will facilitate the exercise of all the gifts of the Spirit throughout the body, working toward the supreme goal of spiritual edification and multiplication. In such circumstances, other new leaders will emerge. On the other hand, dictators in the Lord's work generally preside over sterile assemblies and become little gods hungry to be worshiped and obeyed. The ministry suffers because it is not God's intention that it be carried out by one or two people.

Dynamic, Edifying Ministry, Relevant to Needs

Activity 32 (Goal: event 29): Provide for efficient and relevant teaching to meet the needs of the congregation (figure 37).

Fig. 37

Edifying Teaching Ministry

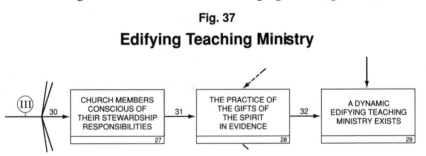

Greek titles used for church leaders in the New Testament tend to be descriptive of function and are often interchangeable. Leaders were to govern the local congregation by example (1 Pet. 5:2–3), minister the Word of God (2 Tim. 4:2), equip believers in the church so that they in turn could build up one another (Eph. 4:11–12), protect the church from false teachers (Acts 20:28–30), and visit the sick and pray for their healing (James 5:14).[19]

Activity 32 in our PERT plan envisions an efficient, Spirit-filled teaching ministry of the Word. Ephesians 4:12 indicates that God expects the body of Christ in its local setting to be "built up." This requires an overall sensitivity to the felt needs of the congregation. The whole counsel of God also must be communicated in the power of the

18. Hesselgrave, *Planting Churches*, 288.
19. Ibid. See also Shenk and Stutzman, *Creating Communities*, 171–72.

Spirit. Fancy homiletical schemes must give way to practical biblical exposition. I have found that an expository homiletical style which endeavors to interpret the meaning of Scripture phrase by phrase, verse by verse will be consistently used by the Holy Spirit in a *wide range* of ministry to meet a variety of needs sensed by those present.

The teaching program of the church should range throughout Scripture, allowing the Spirit to use the various kinds of literature contained therein. Bible school, Sunday services, week-day services, and home Bible study cells should together present a "balanced diet."

Although an evangelistic spirit might well undergird all teaching, those who minister the Word should avoid continuing to evangelize Christians. Normally, the majority of those attending church services in the central place of meeting are already believers. They are hungry for good Bible teaching. They want to know more of God's Word. They truly need to be prepared for everyday Christian living and for witnessing to those outside the fold. Of course, wise preachers and teachers will communicate the Word (even while "teaching") in such a fashion that the gospel will be presented to anyone present who needs to know Christ.

Church planters the world over are recognizing that one of the most productive learning experiences occurs when the church membership, grouped into small cells within geographical proximity of their residences, meet together in homes to sing, to pray, and inductively study God's Word. Each cell meets at its own appointed time once a week, with lay leaders monitoring the meetings. In this way, leadership opportunities are multiplied; family, neighbors and friends are introduced to live Christianity; evangelism occurs, and a wider, more intimate fellowship is enjoyed.[20]

The Practice of Body Life

Activity 33 (Goal: event 30): Continually encourage the members of the church to live as a body (figure 38).

Fig. 38

Living as a Body

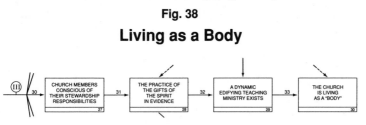

---

20. See activity 19 in our PERT plan for discussion of the evangelistic aspects of small cell groups.

The Apostle Paul was inspired in writing to the Roman, Corinthian, and Ephesian churches to use the analogy of the human body when speaking of their relationship to one another as fellow believers in the church:

> For even as the body is one and yet has many members, and all the members of the body, though they are many, are one body, so also is Christ. For by one Spirit we are all baptized into one body, whether Jews or Greeks, whether slaves or free, and we were all made to drink of one Spirit. For the body is not one member, but many. . . . [and] there are many members, but one body. And the eye cannot say to the hand, "I have no need of you"; or again the head to the feet, "I have no need of you." . . . [T]he members should have the same care for one another. . . . Now you are Christ's body and individually members of it [1 Cor. 12:12–14, 20–21, 25b, 27].

The figure of a healthy body presents a number of valuable insights which harmonize with the New Testament teaching in general. One man who has popularized this in an unprecedented way is Ray C. Stedman. He closes his widely read book, *Body Life*, with the challenge to the church to take Ephesians 4, 1 Corinthians 12 and Romans 12 *seriously*. As that happens, "the Lord of the Church is ready to heal and to bless."[21]

In a newly planted church, those responsible for its growth should seriously follow this Spirit-inspired New Testament analogy. That the church is like a body was clearly taught by the Apostles and has been rediscovered by twentieth-century Christian leaders. To neglect the organic aspects of the church is to effectively quench the power of the Spirit in his edifying ministry. One should pause and consider the disastrous consequences of such negligence. Many pastors wonder why their congregations are sick and dying. Is God's Word truly our only rule of faith and practice; or just those parts *we* choose to make so? This is not an unimportant question.

How then must we take apostolic teaching seriously in this matter of the church living as a body? Here are some seed thoughts gleaned from Stedman:

1. The church is to be a witness to the Christ who lives within her in word, attitude and deed. She must reveal the Christ (Eph. 2:19–22; 3:9, 10, and Acts 1:8).
2. As a body, the healthy church must *maintain* the unity of the Spirit (Eph. 4:3). The differences among members will tend to cause division, but, due to the nature of the gospel, the Spirit

21. Ray C. Stedman, *Body Life* (Glendale, Calif.: Regal, 1972), 143.

recognizes no barriers between men and expects the church to maintain what the Trinity has established (Eph. 4:4–6).

3. Each member of the body must recognize and begin to exercise personal spiritual gift or gifts (as previously explained in activities 31 and 32 of this chain).

4. The offices of apostle, prophet, evangelist, and pastor-teacher should admit that they exist for but one function: *to train, motivate, and undergird the people to do the work of the ministry.*

5. The work of the ministry should consist of evangelizing, teaching, praying, and explaining the times (Luke 4:17–21).

6. To do this, the church membership must know one another closely and intimately enough to be able to bear one another's burdens in ministry to one another through the Word, song and prayer (John 13:34; Gal. 6:2; James 5:16).

7. The ultimate goal: *to be conformed to the image of Jesus Christ* (Rom. 8:9).[22]

A new church will live as a body (PERT event 30) and spiritually take care of itself to the extent that events 27, 28, 29, and 30 are realized. Those responsible for sick and unproductive congregations might well use this set of activities and goals to diagnose their situations to find out just where they are failing to practice God's Word.

22. Ibid., 8–117. See Stedman (and others) for detailed development of these biblical themes.

7

Meaningful Worship

It is always good to stop once in awhile to review what we are saying and to make sure that we are integrating the important aspects of our study into a comprehensible whole. In the case of this book, we must frequently review the set of key goals in figure 6 on page 38. At this stage of our study, we are progressing through the goals which help the church to grow and organize its activities. This logically begins to happen following the birth of the church. We all know that a baby cannot "reproduce": it has to grow and develop to be able to do so. The same is true of a "baby" church; it too has to develop in order to be capable of planting other churches which will in turn plant others.

In our PERT plan in figure 6, there are three groups of goals (networks II, III, and IV) which are arranged to lead to three major objectives. These three objectives are basic to a church that will reproduce itself and plant more churches. The first objective, you will remember from chapter 5, was to lead the church *to live for others*. This is to be accomplished through aggressive evangelism joined with a loving, Christ-like concern for the social needs of the people being reached. This is designated network II in our strategy.

A second major objective concerns what George Peters preferred to call "the inward function of the church."[1] By this we mean that the

---

1. George W. Peters, *A Theology of Church Growth* (Grand Rapids: Zondervan, 1981), 188.

107

church should be led in various ways *to take care of itself*. C. Peter Wagner has helped us dissect this goal to make it more understandable.[2] I have accordingly tried to show this in figure 6 by isolating five internal needs of a developing church: the areas of liturgy or worship, administration, spiritual life, finances, and self-image. All five are elements of network III in our plan. This network concerns the *inner workings* of the congregation—its *personal* fitness for the task of reproduction.

I purposely placed the "spiritual life" of the church in the center of the PERT plan in figure 6 because of its basic importance. Chapter 6 dealt with goals that are fundamental to a credible spiritual life from the standpoint of apostolic Christianity. We now proceed further to study yet another of the five parts of network III, the important subject of liturgy and worship. Peters said that in order to minister to others, which concerned us in network II, "the church must learn to minister to itself and build itself into a quality community."[3] Unfortunately, this is much needed counsel in churches today as they dream of the year 2000 and beyond with the evangelization of the world in their sights.

As we think through the subject of *meaningful worship*, there are at least three events or goals to achieve within the local church. It is perfectly possible in any particular situation that more "events" will become evident. Our plan is flexible throughout in this respect. To help review the big picture, take out the complete PERT chart to refresh your memory.

Elements of Public Worship

R. V. G. Thomson points out that the biblical vocabulary for worship is very rich. Nevertheless, the essential meanings in both Hebrew and Greek center on "service" to God in the sense that his servants bow down in "worship" in "reverential fear and adoring awe and wonder."[4]

Worship in the Old Testament

In his excellent book, *The House Church*, Del Birkey points out that, contrary to what many think today, the Old Testament Scriptures do not support a worship arrangement requiring specially constructed church buildings and elaborate sanctuaries.[5] True, the Old Testament focuses on the problem of worship as a central concern. There were

2. C. Peter Wagner, *Frontiers in Missionary Strategy* (Chicago: Moody, 1971), 163–67.
3. Peters, *A Theology*, 188.
4. R. V. G. Thomson, "Worship," in J. D. Douglas, gen. ed., *The New Bible Dictionary* (Grand Rapids: Eerdmans, 1962).
5. Del Birkey, *The House Church* (Scottdale, Pa.: Herald, 1988), 115.

formal liturgies for both tabernacle and temple. The most formal practices, however, may have been developed nonbiblically and point to the human tendency to be preoccupied with extraneous rituals, putting God in a box. Birkey claims that worshipers were summoned from this preoccupation "to inward experience of renewal."[6]

The first community worship in the Old Testament was in Genesis 4:26 when, in the days of Seth and Enoch, "men began to call on the name of the Lord." Birkey prefers to call this a "house-community." The concept of "God-on-the-move" is born in Abraham's experience as he literally moved out with God. He built altars as declarations of his faith, but he lived in tents. The tabernacle built later by Moses under God's direction intensified this concept of mobility.

The temple, Birkey claims, was not God's idea at all (2 Sam. 7:7), but was nevertheless "cautiously allowed." God would consent to "dwell" in it *if* the people were faithful. Even Solomon, at the dedication (1 Kings 8:27), questions, "But will God indeed dwell on the earth? Behold, heaven and the highest heaven cannot contain Thee, how much less this house which I have built?" God's plan was to "build a house out of David instead."[7]

Solomon's temple was leveled by Nebuchadnezzar, and, even though God later permitted another to be built in its place in the time of Haggai and Zechariah, he assured them, "I am with you. . . . My Spirit is abiding in your midst" (Hag. 2:4–5). "True worship of God happened in every place the truly committed offered pure offerings" (Mal. 1:10–11).[8] The Lord had spoken similarly to Ezekiel in captivity, assuring the prophet that "He Himself had been their real sanctuary all along!"[9] The fact is, as Malachi was inspired to reveal, that genuine worship can only take place when God dwells among his people.

Worship was congregational for the most part in Old Testament times: first in the tabernacle, then in the temple, and finally in synagogue and temple, during and following the captivity. This latter was carried over into the time of Jesus and the early years of the Church, which probably followed the synagogue model.

A Fundamental Problem

Across these centuries one can detect a fundamental problem related to public worship. Its *ritual* or *ceremony* is in tension or conflict with its *spiritual aspects*. The sacrifices, the incense, the priestly blessing, and so forth contributed to ceremonial pageantry. Certainly many Israelites experienced real inward spiritual worship, expressing their

6. Ibid., 116.
7. Ibid., 117.
8. Ibid.
9. Ibid., 118.

love and thankfulness to God by means of public praise in the Psalms and prayers. However, others went through the motions but departed devoid of any personal spiritual benefit or edification. Likewise, people today are attracted by a good religious show which carries little spiritual significance for their personal lives. They have not had an encounter with the living God. They have simply "gone to church." Setting forth the evidence of Matthew 5:23f.; Luke 10:25; John 4:20–24, and James 1:27, Thomson writes:

> Christ participated in both (temple and synagogue), but He always indicated the worship that is the love of the heart towards a heavenly Father. In His teaching, the approach to God through ritual and priestly meditation is not merely unimportant, it is now unnecessary. At last "worship" is true . . . service offered to God not only in terms of temple worship but service to one's fellows.[10]

A fundamental danger which new and mature churches alike must continually preoccupy themselves in avoiding is the form without meaning that too often characterizes so-called "worship" services. Has the service fallen into a rut of ritual and noncommunicating ceremony? Is unwarranted attention being given to the physical surroundings in which worship is conducted?

New Testament Worship

Regarding New Testament era worship, Thomson finds principles in Acts 20:7; 1 Corinthians 11:23–28; Ephesians 5:19, and Colossians 3:16:

> Clearly the day of worship *par excellence* was the Lord's Day . . . [on which] worship was conducted in believers' homes. In such circumstances official ministrants would be unnecessary. Simplicity would be the keynote of these house-church worship services, consisting for the most part of praise, prayer, reading from the Scriptures, and exposition. The love feast, followed by the Lord's Supper, were also common features of Christian worship. But the emphasis throughout would be upon the Spirit, and the inner love and devotion of the heart.[11]

The classic passages on the purity of Christian worship are John 4:23–24, Romans 12:1, and Philippians 3:3. They reveal its inner essence as a genuine expression of inner love and devotion.

Defining Worship Today

Worship may be defined as "the response to God's Spirit in us to that Spirit in Him whereby we answer 'Abba, Father,' deep calling unto

10. Thomson, "Worship."
11. Ibid.

deep."[12] As we worship God, then, we make a loving attempt to pay back a debt that is really unpayable. Worship expresses an attitude of mind. Certainly we are right in insisting that the public worship of God in the community of believers is vital to the Christian's life. In spiritual Christian practice, the ceremonial and the external are of very slight importance.

Activity 21 (Goal: event 19): Endeavor to identify those elements in public services that are not communicating, whether to Christians or to non-Christians (figure 39).

Fig. 39

Public Services Analyzed

I think we have to honestly face the fact that much of our modern congregational religious activity does not result in meaningful encounter with our God. This is sad, very sad when we consider that this should be the reason we come together in his presence. Even in conservative evangelical churches, many are caught in the trap of a sterile formalism. Many missionary church planters tend to take this sterile type of "worship" with them overseas and employ it in new church planting situations in other cultures. The result is no more fruitful there than it was at home.

A number of years ago, Keith Miller wrote:

> Our churches are filled with people who outwardly look contented and at peace but inwardly are crying out for someone to love them. . . . just as they are—confused, frustrated, often frightened, guilty, and often unable to communicate even within their own families. But *other* people in the church *look* so happy and contented that one seldom has the courage to admit his own deep needs before such a self-sufficient group as the average church meeting appears to be.[13]

Wagner comments further that the liturgy of a strong, mature church "is not a carbon copy of that of the mother church. It has intel-

12. Philip Wendell Crannell, "Worship," in James Orr, gen. ed., *The International Standard Bible Encyclopaedia*, rev. ed. (Chicago: Howard-Severance, 1939).
13. Keith Miller,*The Taste of New Wine* (Waco, Tex.: Word, 1965), 22. This is a book with which church planters should be familiar.

lectually examined all things and retained the good. Few liturgical elements can be transferred cross-culturally and still retain their deeper meanings. New liturgy must emerge from the grass roots, since it is intrinsically culture-bound."[14] This is precisely the burden of our concern for the new church as it worships in community. Church planting in Portugal, with the nation's Roman Catholic tradition, presents a challenge. Since Vatican Council II the Roman Church there, as elsewhere, has shown a certain preoccupation with modernizing its public image and enlivening its worship. Church planting efforts in Korea or in the Central African Republic will face other challenges as Christians determine how to conduct public worship.

As evangelicals we might well question whether we are, in effect, speaking a dead language! Does the church service "speak" to the worshiper? If not, why not? Are we "playing church" with form or vocabulary that has little meaning to the average worshiper? These key questions should stimulate necessary reflection and analysis. The church in much of Europe today is dead or dying, partly a result of obvious theological apostasy since their lifeline to truth has been cut, and partly because laity are turned off by well-meaning but sterile evangelical services. They are uninteresting, somehow detached from the felt needs of people and insensitive to the individuals present in the congregation.

Hymns and Music

Take, for instance, the question of hymns and music. Wagner, an experienced church planter in South America, writes:

> The hymnology of the mature church reflects the national or ethnic musical idiom in a recognizable way. It combines good taste with authentic music and is able to strike the balance between reverence and indulgence. Chandu Ray suggests that "When missionaries from western countries came to southeast Asia, they translated the hymns from the German and English languages and paid scant attention to the power of indigenous music, which went with the dance and drama of existing cultures."[15]

Nationals in many lands can testify to the truth of Chandu Ray's words. This is not to say that many of these hymns in their translations do not speak to national believers and unbelievers. It is a warning that better use should be made of the musical idiom of the people with whom we are working. After all, this is what Charles Wesley did in his day, putting Christian lyrics to music he heard sung in the fields by peasants as he rode mile after mile on horseback.

14. Wagner, *Frontiers*, 164.
15. Ibid.

Homiletics and Homiletical Style

The same principle applies to homiletical style in preaching. Having experience in Latin cultures, I speak here from that perspective. The Portuguese and the Spanish are emotional and alive. It would be ill-advised to stand motionless in a public service in Portugal, showing no real feeling in the delivery of a message. A well-known Mexican evangelist, brother Juan Isais, visited Portugal in the late 1960s. We were mobilizing the nation's evangelicals for an Evangelism-in-Depth program, traveling from church to church. Juan's key word in his native Spanish was *movimiento*, meaning "Get moving!" He was a living example of *movimiento*—all over the platform when he spoke. The people loved it. They were deeply moved because he was communicating, reaching the people with the message of revival and action in Christian witnessing. There is no "right style" in preaching. If it is communicating the truths of the Word of God, it is right. It is wrong when it does not communicate these truths. Wagner and others are correct when they say that the homiletical style used in a mature church will have been freely adapted to the local cultural patterns.[16]

If we are serious about worship and how the message is coming across, it is good to try to find out what the members of the church think about the services. Do they have any helpful ideas to improve the public meetings? Think of some way to allow them to freely reveal their opinions. Churches that have a congregational form of government are more easily able to do this. Of course, the leaders of the church must be sincerely interested to hear and also prepared for criticism and possible change.

Necessary Changes to Improve Worship

Activity 22 (Goal: event 20): Decide how to improve communication in the public worship services (figure 40).

Fig. 40
Satisfactory Communication

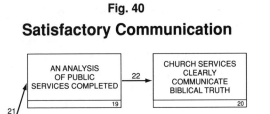

An explanation of what is meant by "communication" is in order. The word itself is derived from the Latin *communis* ("common"), so it

16. Ibid., 207.

is obvious that to have communication with someone we must establish a certain "commonness" with them. Speaking in terms of communication theory, "that 'commonness' is to be found in mutually shared codes."[17] When applied to church planting and especially to public services, this means that our objective should be to decide which codes are truly *mutually shared*.

The elliptical design in figure 41 illustrates the essential dynamics of the communication process as understood by Hesselgrave.[18] Note that the *source* of the communication can be primary, secondary, or tertiary, depending upon how it received the message. A missionary or evangelist is a secondary source, the primary one being the biblical writer. The *encoding* process seeks to put the message into some kind of coded system able to transfer the meaning accurately to the context of the one who is to receive it. This receiving person is the *respondent* or *receptor*. The respondent *decodes* the message by interpreting it for himself. Messages are encoded by means of *verbal codes* (either spoken or written) or *nonverbal codes* (such as by gestures, proper behavior, music, or drama). Hesselgrave points out that the message "never exists in the sense of having an independent existence. *Its existence is in the source*, in the encoded form, perceived by the respondent and decoded by the respondent. Much misunderstanding would be averted if we could but grasp the truth that *in a very real sense messages are in human beings*—in sources and receptors—not in words or pictures or acts."[19]

In figure 41, note that the *medium* of communication is "the means by which messages in the forms of verbal and non-verbal codes are conveyed to respondents."[20] It can be *simple media*: written autographs, original diagrams; or *syndetic media* requiring multiple skills: such as books, films, radio, television, and drama.

Feedback is a well-known phenomenon in the realm of microphones and amplifying equipment. Here it is employed to refer to the need for response of information back to the encoder, because true communication is always two-way. For good communication to occur the source needs to know at least three things about the receptors:

1. Was the other person listening?
2. Did the receptor think about what was heard?
3. What did the receptor think?

17. David J. Hesselgrave, *Communicating Christ Cross-Culturally* (Grand Rapids: Zondervan, 1978), 31. The author has made a most valuable contribution to missionary church planters in this excellent work.
18. Ibid., 28-37.
19. Ibid., 29. Emphasis author's.
20. Ibid., 34.

Fig. 41

The Process of Communication

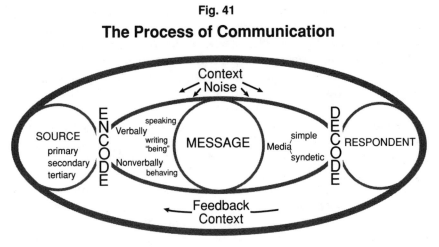

David J. Hesselgrave, *Communicating Christ Cross-Culturally*
(Grand Rapids: Zondervan, 1978), 37.

It is easy to see that this feedback is really necessary. Otherwise, how is the source to adjust to the *real* understanding and reactions of the respondents as communication continues?[21]

In figure 41 *noise* includes all factors that adversely affect communication. Their influence must be reduced if communication is to be improved. Finally, there is a *context* to all communication. The contexts of messages and those who hear them must be reckoned with, no matter what form the communication takes. All of this has a direct bearing upon church planting in its initial and growth stages. This is especially true when ministry is carried out in cross-cultural situations.

Communication—Church Services

Chandu Ray's remark about missionary translations of hymns from German and English into the languages of southeast Asia is true in other areas as well. A study of Portuguese evangelical hymn books, for example, found one hymnal that is widely used, yet only two of its 194 composers are of Portuguese origin. Of the eighty-three authors listed, only about one-half are Portuguese. If one does not understand the words and expressions used in hymns, how is one to worship intelligently?

One reason there are so many attempts to make the English Bible more readable is that people do not understand nor relate to archaic language translations not many centuries or even decades old. Language and thought have changed rapidly in the United States

21. Ibid., 35.

and England. The same is true in Germany, the Netherlands, France, and a multitude of other countries. For example, the *Living Bible* paraphrase in a revised Dutch edition, *Het Boek*, produced a revival in Bible reading in the Netherlands. Within five months of its appearance it sold 50,000 copies and entered its third edition. Why? Both pastors and common people found it to be captivating reading. They understood what they read. It communicated!

Our preaching often uses expressions that come out of a theological, doctrinal, and historical background far removed from the way of life of our audiences. The source must concern himself with the respondent. It is important to understand and apply the facts of the communication process in our worship services as well as in all congregational interchange. These and other elements in church services call for attention as we ask ourselves: Are we communicating effectively?

The burden, therefore, in each local church context is to achieve that "commonness" whereby the triune God is actually experienced in his fullness by those who are his people. The unique Word of God should be encoded, transmitted, and decoded in the communication process through Spirit-anointed music, the transmission of the inspired Scriptures, and Spirit-filled preaching. This should pave the way for "mutually shared codes" and the "commonness" essential for meaningful worship. The result should be spiritual communication. Going back for a moment to activity 21, the analysis of public services, it is reasonable to expect that those responsible for ministry in the church will be vitally interested in obtaining the best possible feedback from the receptors—the congregation—to determine how to improve communication.

What are some simple rules to keep in mind while planning the congregational worship of the local church?

1. Remember that God wants to speak to *each person* in the audience. He will do so through other persons in the "body," as well as from the pulpit.
2. Basic gospel truth must be clearly communicated, both verbally and nonverbally. Even Bible exposition can evangelize if the simple elements of the good news are present. The Spirit sovereignly uses the Word to accomplish his purposes with both the saved and unsaved in the same meeting.
3. Early believers met together, according to Luke, to worship the Lord, to pray for one another and for the ministry, to fellowship at the Lord's table, to be instructed and built up in the faith, to help those in need with their material means, and to carry out their commission from the Lord (Acts 2:41–47; Gal. 6:2). Do our church gatherings achieve these results?
4. Does the Holy Spirit have freedom in each service? Paul wrote to

the Thessalonian church, "Do not quench the Spirit" (1 Thess. 5:19). There is a reason for this command. *He* is the Great Communicator! So many churches today are quenching the Spirit in the name of doing everything decently and in order.

5. Does each church service further the feeling of brotherhood? Are those present a loving family of God? In other words, do those present *act out* their oneness with Christ, their Lord? (Phil. 2:1–4; Eph. 2:19).

6. Is the language used in the service understandable? Is God's message understood?

7. Are the leaders absolutely clear as to the goals of the service?

Careful attention to these vitally important matters is bound to revolutionize our attitudes with respect to public meetings, how we plan for them, and how we conduct them.

Activity 23 (Goal: event 21): Hold services, keeping activities 21 and 22 in mind (figure 42).

Fig. 42

Services Full of Meaning

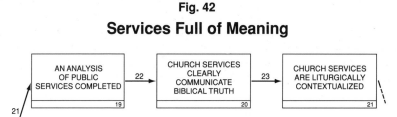

Our burden throughout this chapter has been to discern how to worship together in such a fashion that the time spent as a congregation speaks to all of us in a deeply meaningful manner. In our day-to-day physical existence, watching our health and general well-being is normally a constant preoccupation. We accept this as life. Why should it be so different in the spiritual realm in the local church? Spiritual life also goes on from day to day; if we are not alert to what has been said here a certain hardness gradually builds in the congregation. Real spiritual exchange and communication is slowly choked off until all that is left is a kind of empty liturgical ritual. Howard A. Snyder relates that it is rare to find open, winsome intimacy within the institutionalized church, "where masks are dropped, honesty prevails, and there is that sense of communication and community beyond the human— where there is literally the fellowship of and in the Holy Spirit."[22]

22. Howard Snyder, *The Problem of Wine Skins: Church Structure in a Technological Age* (Downers Grove, Ill.: Inter-Varsity, 1975), 89-90. This is an excellent resource for church planters.

Every church gathering presents a new set of conditions. Those in leadership roles must remain *flexible*, allowing the Spirit freedom to alter a previously planned and even printed order of service. Leaders must be *sensitive* to what is actually happening in the congregation as well as in the pulpit. The close informality of the early house church gatherings should be sought, for priestly, liturgical stiffness has a way of making prisoners of the audience. In Christian worship all should become one before God in a happy, joyful service of love and adoration. Who says that women can't take part? Who says the youth cannot take important parts? Who says there is no time for someone who has had a vibrant spiritual experience to testify of this to the brethren? Leadership in the local church must allow the Spirit to edify the congregation through the gifts he has bestowed on its members. A cold, programed leader can literally quench the Spirit, extinguishing the spiritual fire that God wants to burn in the hearts of his people.

Another factor of effective worship is that leaders should *not* allow themselves to be overwhelmed by the size of the congregation, whether large or small. The Lord wants to meet *each* one present. No matter what the number, contagious feelings of enthusiasm, thanksgiving, koinonia, holy joy, and adoration should be cultivated (Matt. 18:20; Eph. 5:19–20; Phil. 4:4; Col. 3:12–17). Certainly prayer should permeate the meeting where God's people are gathered. All must be reminded that it is God we worship and his blessing we seek as we bow in a spirit of reverent service before him.

8

Church Administration

In chapter 2 I attempted to apply to church planting some basic principles of sound management advocated by leading consultants. Even though administration is a gift of the Spirit (Rom. 12:8; 1 Cor. 12:28), it needs to be developed because it is a learned skill.[1] Considering the question of how to administer the affairs of a new local church, we call attention to another essential objective on the path to achieving "a church that takes care of itself" (PERT event 42).

A new church must grow in its *spiritual life* and in *meaningful worship*, but it must also grow in an *orderly, disciplined fashion*. Otherwise, confusion and frustration will sap the spiritual energy needed to reach our long-range goal. I am convinced that one reason so many evangelical churches have succumbed to a state of practical dictatorship is that they were never led to believe that anything else was possible or acceptable. As you reflect on this, keep in mind always what was presented in chapter 6 with regard to stewardship, spiritual gifts, and body life. Remember that all the activities and events we discuss in PERT networks II, III, and IV concerning the growth and organization of the church are intimately interrelated and must be fully integrated.

One of the basic elements David J. Hesselgrave mentions in his

1. Edward R. Dayton and David A. Fraser, *Planning Strategies for World Evangelization* (Grand Rapids: Eerdmans, 1980), 43.

119

"Pauline Cycle," regarding permanent organization, concerns the task "Leadership Consecrated" (see figure 1). Hesselgrave explains that "permanent organization of the church should be established that is scriptural, functional, effective, and expandable."[2] Expandable means partly that leadership can adapt to the changes in a growing church. The networks of our plan develop depth as the church grows over time. The church is a living organism.

Activities for the Life and Ministry of the Church

Activity 24 (Goal: event 22): Determine what internal and external activities are necessary for the life of the church (figure 43).

Fig. 43
Activities Study Completed

As a "baby" church begins to grow, certain administrative needs will surface as they did in the Jerusalem church. True, they were small congregations, meeting in houses much of the time. Even so, Luke records a rather dramatic crisis in Acts 6 which demanded a solution if the ministry of the Word was to advance. A similar crisis occurred some years ago in a large denominational church in Lisbon, Portugal. The pastor of a congregation of more than 600 members complained to me one day that he had to do everything—even clean the toilets in the building! He was an excellent evangelist and expositor of the Word, but he was apparently blind to what we are about to say. When today's spiritual leaders allow themselves to be made directly responsible for the execution of practically every imaginable job in the local church, no one should be surprised when they fail.

Jethro's advice to Moses (Exod. 18:13–27) as well as the wise decision of the twelve (Acts 6:2–4) resulted in freeing both for the service to which they were called and for which they were gifted by the Spirit. In the case of the apostles, Acts 6:7 relates how the church continued to grow. There is evidence, as things progressed in the church life of the New Testament period, that new needs were met in like fashion: new posts of service were created. Some offices took on new specific

2. David J. Hesselgrave, *Planting Churches Cross-Culturally: A Guide for Home and Foreign Missions* (Grand Rapids: Baker Book House, 1980), 351.

meanings which evolved as needs arose. Missionary statesman Roland Allen wrote: "There was order in the expansion: . . . ministers were appointed from among themselves, presbyter bishops or bishops, who in turn could organize and bring into unity of the visible Church any new group of Christians in their neighborhood."[3]

We are talking about leaders seeking to be spiritually alert or aware of the organizational and administrative changes needed in the growing church. We must always remember that the Holy Spirit administers the work of the Godhead among humanity and so must be vitally involved in all the administration of Christ's body. The first of what came to be called deacons in Acts 6 were to be men "full of the Spirit." Under the guidance of the Spirit, one of the important specific functions of elders in the New Testament era was to *govern* the congregation (1 Tim. 5:17), not by lording (*katakurieuontes*) over it but by example (*tupoi*, 1 Pet. 5:3).

Questions need to be asked. For example: what specific services does the congregation require? What is needed administratively in order to carry on meaningful public worship? Is there property to maintain? What about the administration of the Sunday school? How about the structures for effective evangelism and caring social involvement? In the case of multiple house-churches, how are they to relate to each other and what about their structure as parts of the whole? Luke doesn't record all of this about the works of Jerusalem, Corinth, Ephesus, Philippi or Thessalonica, but obviously something was done. Titus, Silas and Timothy were involved with others in helping the local churches with administrative counsel. One wonders what all was in Paul's mind when he told Titus to "set in order what remains" (Titus 1:5). Normally, depending upon the size of the congregation, dozens of specific jobs will be recognized. They are really needed. Activity 24 in our PERT plan will proceed to list these "jobs" and to logically relate them to one another.

One evangelical pastor in Portugal invited his church officers and congregation of about 120 to participate in an unusual project. They were to analyze the way the church operated in order to improve, if possible, their ministry. About eighteen to twenty assembled each Friday night (not always the same people) at the house the church rented for its meetings. The planners first wrote down as many different tasks as they could think of that were being done in the church by its members. Every task from serving as an usher to serving as a gardener was listed. On the wall the pastor then taped these pieces of paper. There were suggestions from the group as to how to relate the

3. Roland Allen, *Spontaneous Expansion of the Church and the Causes Which Hinder It* (Grand Rapids: Eerdmans, 1962), 7.

various tasks or jobs. After a few weeks, jobs were satisfactorily grouped in twelve "departments" of church life. Then those meeting tried to relate these departments to one another. Finally, after months of work, organization had been studied and refined and it was decided that the head of each of these departments would be a member of a team-centered administrative board (see figure 44).[4] This board meets once a month. Each department head reports to the board about the life of the church under his or her care, projects plans for the future month or months, and, where advisable, seeks the cooperation of the other departments in the coordination of activities. Matters that involve the decision of the whole congregation are presented in quarterly business meetings or in specially called meetings. In the Portuguese scene, the pastor is expected to chair such a board. However, in this setup he certainly cannot fall into a position of dictatorship or one-man-ship. This careful organization began a growth pattern in that church which has resulted in the planting of several other churches.

Fig. 44
Team-centered Administration

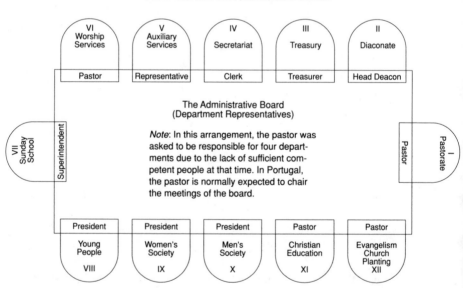

4. For an excellent presentation of organization structure and team-centered organization see Kenneth K. Kilinski and Jerry C. Wofford, *Organization and Leadership in the Local Church* (Grand Rapids: Zondervan, 1973), 142–64. See also Olan Hendrix, *Management and the Christian Worker* (Manila, Philippines: Living Books For All, 1970), 74–107.

"Baby" congregations will have fewer administrative needs than larger bodies, but no church, whatever its size, should be loaded with administrative machinery that it does not need. Solutions should be strictly *functional*. Recognized needs should be promptly cared for as exemplified in Acts 6.

Job Descriptions

Activity 25 (Goal: event 23): Write a job description for each needed task or job in the church life (figure 45).

Fig. 45

Job Descriptions Ready

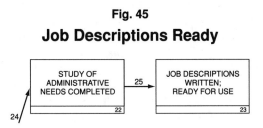

Several years ago, while I was visiting a large church in the midwestern United States, I was approached by a dear man who said, "I have just been elected to be a deacon of our church, but I'm somewhat embarrassed. I really don't know what is expected of me. You're a missionary. Could you help me?" Certainly this is not an isolated case. Not too long ago, during interviews with pastors in Portugal, I discovered that only 30 percent use any form of job description as a basis for determining a person's qualifications for a specific position of responsibility. After talking with pastors and laymen, I feel strongly that laymen as well as salaried personnel in churches are eager to know exactly what is expected of them, no matter what the service is that they are chosen to perform.

Job descriptions serve several purposes for the church:

1. They provide a vehicle for structuring the organization of the church by allowing the assignment of responsibility.
2. They clarify formal communication channels and the reporting relationships among leaders and workers.
3. They can be used to identify the qualifications required for the job and to orient the person who is placed in the job.
4. They can be useful in training a person to do the job, motivating the person to fulfil its demands, defining goals for future action, and setting out an understanding of jurisdiction of the activities.[5]

5. Kilinski and Wofford, *Organization*, 168–69.

I turn again to one of the most useful little volumes with regard to management, *Management and the Christian Worker* by Olan Hendrix. In an excellent, concise treatment of job descriptions he writes that they define both our work and our reason for being in the organization.[6] "A job description helps our boss to know what we are doing. It helps us to know what he expects of us, and it lets people around us know what we are doing. Likewise, we know why their jobs exist."[7]

Writing the Job Description

The church I mentioned identified some sixty-nine tasks and organized them into departments. Then the pastor led the planners through the exercise of writing job descriptions for each task. It took several weeks to do this because discussion of further suggestions kept refining the copy. Sunday school teachers worked on theirs. Deacons worked on theirs. The pastor worked on his. The group met to discuss each.

The purpose of activity 25, then, is to follow through and to write descriptions of all the tasks identified. These descriptions should follow a format. Hendrix said that "the more innovative, creative, imaginative the job, the greater the need for the job description but the more difficult to write."[8] The kind of format used is unimportant so long as it covers the essential information. Hendrix suggests the following parts for a job description:

Job title. Accurately describe the service to be performed—"pastor," "deacon," "elder," "superintendent of the Sunday school," "usher."

Name. The name of the person chosen for this job. At only two points should the name of the individual who will occupy the position appear—at the top of the sheet and in a statement on training and development.[9]

Date. Every job description should carry the date when it was written or revised. Normally job descriptions should be reviewed and updated at least once a year.

Part 1: the job summary. What is the end result which the job exists to accomplish? This summary "is the most difficult thing to write in all of the job description. It must be measurable, definitive, and specific."[10]

Part 2: the job duties. There should be a list of the exact activities required to accomplish the job goal stated in the summary. Here

6. Hendrix, *Management*, 108–18.
7. Ibid., 109.
8. Ibid.
9. Ibid., 112.
10. Ibid., 114.

the distinction between similar jobs can be clarified. Responsibilities should be listed in such a way that overlap is eliminated. Each job described carries its own peculiar responsibilities.

Part 3: organizational relationships. Hendrix reminds us that "organizational relationships extend in four directions: up, down, and sideways in both directions."[11] In this regard there are two important words to remember: *to* and *for.* Each person occupying a job is responsible *to* (up) someone and *for* (down) someone. In the team-centered administration shown in figure 44, the president of the young people is responsible *to* the administrative board and *for* the remaining officers of the young people's society. There also are "sideways" relationships with the other members of the board.

Part 4: qualifications. This is what the person should ideally be and know in order to most effectively accomplish the job summary. With clear, realistic qualifications the church can judge whether a person fills the description.

Part 5: training and development. At this point the job description must be personalized to fit the needs of the person. Training and development can make this man or woman qualified, so what is needed and how can it be obtained? The person involved should work with others to develop a mutually acceptable plan with a specific program and schedule. In the case of a Sunday school teacher, for instance, it could be some specific education course that would be taken by a certain date.[12]

Who writes a job description? Kenneth K. Kilinski and Jerry C. Wofford suggest that the one who is doing the job knows it best and should be the one to describe it or at least make a heavy contribution to describing it.[13]

The local church is God's business. We will, therefore, want to take every precaution, above all else, that those who serve in any capacity have *spiritual* qualifications. This was true in Acts 6:3, in Acts 13:1–4 and in Paul's "job descriptions" for elders and deacons to be sent to Timothy and Titus (1 Tim. 3:1–13 and Titus 1:5–9). Even so, there are those who get into positions of authority who are not worthy. This occurred in the church John refers to in 3 John 9–10. The points Paul makes must be clearly expressed in writing with the other qualifications of a modern job description. Local churches today suffer untold hardship and irreparable damage at the hands of those who appear to be highly qualified but who woefully lack spiritual fiber.

11. Ibid., 115.
12. Ibid., 116–17.
13. Kilinski and Wofford, *Organization*, 169.

Selection and Training of Those Who Will Serve

Activity 26 (Goal: event 25): Make certain that each person who accepts a particular job understands the respective job description and its implications (figure 46).

Fig. 46

Members Instructed and Functioning

It is not enough to write the job descriptions: those who are chosen to serve in the various capacities must be introduced to their specific responsibilities. Two of the main reasons people are not functioning efficiently in the jobs assigned to them in the local church are that they do not really know *how* to do what is assigned to them, or they do not know exactly *what* is expected of them.

Good implementation of the above demands patience, patience, and more patience from those who lead. In countries with a rather high incidence of illiteracy and an accompanying low level of educational achievement we must encourage and help people to qualify and function in the church body. All the effort will pay off as God's Spirit achieves his goals in and through the "body." Give people a chance to grow. Give them a chance to make mistakes without being shamed. Give them a chance to make corrections, and to joyfully succeed in their particular service for the Master. Praise work well done. Encourage people when they realize their work is not well done. One of the great joys of the ministry is to see people come out of their shells to serve God and their brethren in the body.

There have been significant breakthroughs in local church leadership development programs.[14] Church planters and local church leaders cannot know too much about this vital element in the achieving of our long-range goal of reproduction.

Revision of the Church Constitution During Growth

Activity 28 (Goal: event 24): Revise the church constitution as needed according to growth of church (figure 47).

14. The Biblical Institute of Leadership Development, Ontario Bible Church, 4707 Hutchison, Ames, Iowa 50010, offers information on many of these programs.

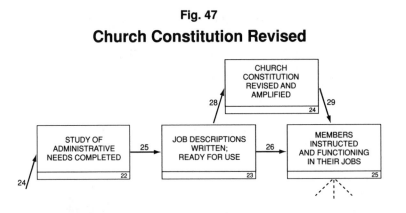

Fig. 47

Church Constitution Revised

While discussing the initial organization of the new church in chapter 4, the "Pioneer Period," I mentioned that the church planting team often takes the initiative to suggest to the organizing nucleus an initial basic church constitution. The contents of such a document will vary according to doctrinal convictions and the organizational principles which govern the evangelical group that sponsors the team.

Missiologist Hesselgrave speaks forcefully about church polity and organization as it relates to culture, maintaining that if a church government takes a form that is foreign to the target culture it will either "adapt functionally to local ways of governance, or it will greatly impede the growth of the church."[15] Having given this warning, however, he strongly advises that a "model constitution" be proposed by the sponsors of the new church. The charter members should be oriented to the fact that they will be able to revise it according to their needs later. Actually it is a tremendous help to the baby congregation to relieve them at the beginning of this arduous task.[16]

It is in order here at least to give the "bare bones" of a model constitution for the benefit of anyone who might not have had the task of working on one. The following are eleven generic article headings that appear in one current church constitution in Portugal.

Article I	The Name and Location
Article II	The Purpose
Article III	The Doctrinal Statement
Article IV	The Church Covenant
Article V	The Government of the Church
Article VI	The Members
Article VII	The Officers

15. Hesselgrave, *Planting Churches*, 367.
16. Ibid., 368–69.

Of special interest in such a constitution is the spirit of the following church covenant from a new church planted in Illinois, which seems to embody much of what we have been saying in chapters 6, 7, and 8. I reproduce it in full.

CHURCH COVENANT

Having been led, as we believe, by the Spirit of God to receive Jesus Christ as Savior and Lord, and having been baptized in the name of the triune God (Father, Son and Holy Spirit) on the profession of our faith in Him, we do solemnly and joyfully enter into this covenant with one another in the presence of God and of His witnesses.

WE SOLEMNLY COVENANT to join together in Christian love and fellowship, praying for and ministering to each other as fellow members in His Body, helping each other in sickness and in difficulties, comforting each other in sorrow, being sensitive to the hurts and needs of one another, and mutually building up the Body in knowledge, holiness, and godly living.

WE SOLEMNLY COVENANT to participate actively in the ministry of this church, finding our specific places of responsibility in the Body and utilizing the spiritual gifts with which God has endowed each of us, and becoming meaningfully involved in the worship, work, and witness to which God has called us.

WE SOLEMNLY COVENANT to strive for the qualitative and quantitative growth and the ever-widening missionary outreach of this church in light of the sobering task committed to us in the Great Commission of our Lord to "make disciples of all nations."

WE SOLEMNLY COVENANT to give cheerfully and regularly of our resources to this church, thus sharing in its financial obligations and supporting its evangelistic and missionary outreach.

WE SOLEMNLY COVENANT to maintain personal and family devotions, to recognize Christ as the center of our family life and witness, and to bring up our children in the nurture and admonition of the Lord, so that they in turn will take their individual places of responsibility in the church family.

WE FURTHER COVENANT that in the event God leads us elsewhere, we will unite as soon as possible with another church of like faith and practice, where we can carry out the spirit of this covenant in keeping with the teaching of God's Word.

Legal Registration

This is a difficult hurdle in many countries where the evangelicals are a tiny minority of the population. Every effort should be made following the organization of the church (see event 12 in figure 6) to go through the process of registering the church with the government and thereby to achieve what could be called "legal personality." The legal statutes required for this process will eventually, of necessity, require changes in the church constitution.

Congregational Approval of Revisions

> *Activity 29 (Goal: event 25):* Secure congregational approval of the constitutional revisions and provide copies for members (figure 47).

The church constitution should regulate the day-to-day life of the church family. Every member of this family should be informed about its contents. Candidates for membership should not be admitted to the church unless they fully agree with its articles. In churches with either a congregational or a presbyterian form of government the local church must adopt the constitution and approve any revisions. Activity 29 of our PERT plan covers this. It is advisable that each church member receive a copy of the new document after each revision. Each revision should carry the date of its acceptance by the church assembly.

You will note on the complete PERT plan that event 25 is connected by broken lines to events 28, 29, and 30. It is a graphic reminder that the spiritual life of the church is directly related to and is also dependent upon members who are instructed and functioning in their respective places of service.

Annual Revision of Job Descriptions

> *Activity 27 (Goal: event 26):* Periodically revise the job descriptions to keep them current (figure 48).

Fig. 48

Adequate Church Administration

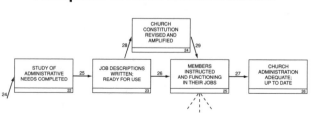

PERT activity 27 places emphasis on the need to keep church administration current. Hendrix insists that a job description that has not been kept up to date can do more harm than good.[17]

We have now discussed three of the five goals which describe a church that takes care of itself. Chapters 9 and 10 will cover the remaining two.

17. Hendrix, *Management*, 108–9.

9

Finances

Financial independence and responsibility are fundamental to healthy adulthood. I think we all would admit that we are not favorably impressed by someone who has reached physical adulthood but who still acts like a child when it comes to finances—one who is forever asking dad and mom for money or who is "over his ears" in unmet obligations. We say that such a child simply has not "grown up." We don't want our children to be that way.

For the same reasons I would say that any sponsor of a new church planting effort, whether a local church, an association of churches, or a foreign mission board, does a great disservice to the new church by continuing financial support that is not governed by a well-thought-out, realistic plan. Such a plan will move the church as rapidly as possible toward financial independence. In southern Europe, one of the factors which have suffocated the multiplication of churches and church growth in general has been financial dependence. Remember our long-range PERT goal. We cannot settle for anything less than a mature church, able and motivated to plant more churches.

In this chapter I would like to develop the fourth subnetwork of network III in our PERT plan. Our goal here is *a financially self-supporting church* (event 33). This is a fundamental indigenous principle; a church that is not financially independent cannot be thought of as taking care of itself (event 42).

Setting Realistic Financial Goals

In the formal organization of the new church discussed in chapter 4 under activity 11, financial prospects are often an important consideration. This depends upon each local situation. In some cases, those sponsoring the new work make the initial suggestions as to how the necessary funds are to be provided. Our experience has been that as the "baby" congregation begins to gather for fellowship and the group grows, obvious financial needs become apparent to those gathered. Under these conditions, the believers will offer their contributions because they feel involved and responsible to help. In one experience, where the church was begun in the home of a Christian couple, the husband made the first offering, even though we were meeting in his home and the expenses were minimal.

There are cases where space must be rented or purchased for the growing congregation. In other strategies, the size is purposely limited in an *oikos* system of small, local house churches. In this way huge building rents and financial overhead are avoided. Whatever the situation, those involved tend to recognize the need for expenditures. In this initial stage, the team and the first converts can together determine what should be included in the first budget. It will probably consist of a simple list of anticipated expenses for the coming year, as well as an estimate of what can be expected in receipts or contributions.

Some undoubtedly will disagree with what I am about to say. They sincerely believe "the pump must be primed in order to draw water." In our context, the thought is that considerable financial outlay is necessary if eventually we are to have a viable church in the area. In Latin cultures where Rome has been dominating for centuries, or in Muslim cultures or Buddhist lands where structures have been fundamental to the exercise of worship, there is a strong conviction among many national evangelicals that buildings are extremely important in order to have a *visible* presence.

I believe the alternative to this conviction lies in our understanding of the long-range goal of our church planting strategy. Charles Brock urges church planters to "think reproducible" in everything that is done, financially and in other aspects of the strategy. New Christians normally follow their leaders. They learn by what is done, as well as by what is verbally taught. This is a bit frightening. The apostle Paul actually instructed the Philippian believers to do this when he wrote, "join in following my example, and observe those who walk according to the pattern you have in us. . . . The things you have learned and received and heard and seen in me, practice these things" (Phil. 3:17; 4:9).

Once we are gone from the scene as a team or as missionaries—once the foreign or outside funds are no longer available—will the church members themselves be able and motivated to repeat in new places what we have left as an example? Or will they throw up their hands and consider it an impossibility? Can small Italian congregations finance their own buildings to the tune of hundreds of thousands of dollars? Can we hope for the multiplication of thousands of needed congregations in a country like Italy or Spain or Portugal using such a model before the nationals? We will have taught them by our own example that you need expensive buildings and some source of finance beyond the local potential in order to have a viable church planting operation. The fact is that we do not need such a facade any more than Paul did! It is a blind alley. It is not the strategy that is likely to facilitate the mass reproduction of new local churches worldwide, which is the crying need in missionary outreach.

I feel strongly that *extreme caution* is in order in the matter of finances. It is most unwise, assuming our final PERT goal, for sponsors to overload a new church with unwarranted financial debts for equipment and property, debts that cannot help but divert its attention and limited resources from the goal to plant other needed churches. American evangelicals have seen this happen in the United States in huge building programs that stymie ministry. Mission programs are set back and the members selfishly enjoy comforts and facilities which in themselves express the lack of vision for reproduction that is the heart of the book of Acts and the Great Commission. *Getting the gospel out into the world and planting new churches is not an extracurricular activity or an option for any Bible believing congregation.* It is an imperative. Unfortunately, we Americans are engaged in exporting to the mission field the sickness which afflicts our home situations.

Once a young church becomes accustomed to employing practically all of its receipts to pay off debts imposed upon it by such methodology, it will be extremely difficult for it to ever be able truly to "live for others" (network II), which is one of the essential elements for reproduction. Donald A. McGavran's prophetic call for the planting of a multitude of new churches throughout the world and the reaching into every people group means that we must avoid this financial dead end. David J. Hesselgrave's reflections are appropriate here as he comments on Roland Allen's strong stand against financing property and other large investments in missions enterprises.

There is a tendency in some situations to allow the church-planting effort to become primarily a financial operation. This is one of the concerns of Roland Allen. He feels that we greatly retard the multiplication of new churches if missionary work becomes a secular operation and finances the chief concern. His reasoning is not difficult to follow. Taking a long look at the apostolic churches he concludes that we are far removed from apostolic practice. In the New Testament period every province and every church was financially independent and assumed obligation for its own teachers and poor. Modern practice in founding churches is to begin by securing a dwelling for the church-planter, some land for a building, necessary equipment for the church, and so forth. Consequently, the planting of churches early becomes a basically "secular business" (Allen's phrase) involving negotiations for real estate, agreements with contractors, and supervision of construction as well as the raising of funds for the entire operation. In this we are as far removed from apostolic practice in action as we are in time.[1]

Hesselgrave further adds that when "church planting and renewal cannot occur without the endless importation of foreign funds, and when church-planters become first 'ministers of finance' and only secondarily 'ministers of the Word,' we have strayed from New Testament principles and have jeopardized the future of our mission in the world."[2]

Activity 34 (Goal: event 31): Establish realistic financial goals that the church can achieve with its own contributions (figure 49).

Fig. 49

A Realistic Budget

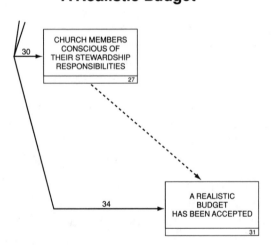

This discussion is closely related to chapter 6 and to the whole question of stewardship. On the complete PERT plan this relationship is indicated by a broken line between events 27 and 31. Spiritual matu-

1. David J. Hesselgrave, *Planting Churches Cross-Culturally* (Grand Rapids: Baker, 1980), 341–42. His reference is to Roland Allen, *Missionary Methods: St. Paul's or Ours?* (Grand Rapids: Eerdmans, 1962), 49–61.
2. Ibid., 342.

rity is an integral factor in the realization of Christian financial responsibility. This again shows the necessity for a *balanced* emphasis during the entire period of growth and organization. Financial independence will always be just beyond the reach of those churches whose members have not become good Christian stewards. The same is true in older established congregations: Their interest in evangelism, in church planting, and in extending their witness to the uttermost parts of the earth will be in proportion to the number of their members who are living according to the standards of Christian biblical stewardship.

The Budget

A budget is defined as "a plan or schedule adjusting expenses during a certain period to estimated or fixed income for that period."[3] A recent survey of church planters (from eight different evangelical groups) indicated that only 42 percent of the churches they plant regulate their expenditures through a budget approved by the church. This can mean that the people of these churches where members are not consulted are in the dark as to what is going on with the financial expenditures. Such is not healthy nor desirable. Our God is a God of order in all that he does. As his people and his body we should do all in our power to avoid confusion and to foster open accountability, especially in financial matters.

What Determines the Budget?

What are realistic financial goals? How does the church determine its budget? The answer is simple: The *needs* of the church should dictate the budget figures. Kenneth K. Kilinski and Jerry C. Wofford stress the faith principles at work here:

> If we believe that Philippians 4:19 means that God will supply all of our needs collectively as well as individually, then after careful, prayerful consideration, our needs should dictate the budget figure. . . . It has been our experience that when we realistically investigate our needs and are willing to trust God to meet them, it is an exciting adventure to establish something with Him which He in turn has promised to do.[4]

Writing from the North American perspective, F. Jack Redford speaks to a problem of many other cultural contexts when he sees budget needs in the new church "clustered around four considerations:

3. "Budget" in *Webster's New World Dictionary*, College ed. (1956).
4. Kenneth K. Kilinski and Jerry C. Wofford, *Organization and Leadership in the Local Church* (Grand Rapids: Zondervan, 1973), 198.

temporary meeting place, leadership, types of ministries to the community, and a permanent location for the new work."[5]

Realistic Budget Figures

One practical way to arrive at realistic budget figures is to work through each department of the new church. As is shown in figure 44 in chapter 8 (page 122), each department should prayerfully project its own needs for the coming year. The deacons, the Sunday school, the young people, and other groups should make budgets. These are then totaled and presented at an assembly of members for their final consideration and approval. In most churches this is done sometime in October or November and takes effect January 1.

Certainly a realistic budget should not ignore the relative potential of the congregation. Ideally, budgets should not be calculated to spend other people's funds! On the other hand, we must not underestimate God. As needs and challenges arise, he stretches the faith of local believers and enables them to contribute much more than they could ask or think. Many times our faith is far too small. We can and should trust God for more than our eyes can see. Nevertheless, I strongly advise that a church make a serious effort to match need with foreseen potential in preparing its operating budget. In so doing, it should believe God will supply through dedicated financial stewardship.

Accounting and Reporting

Kilinski and Wofford observe that, in the context of finances, establishing a budget is only half of the story. "The other half is an *adequate* accounting and reporting system which is absolutely necessary if we are to do all things 'properly and in an orderly manner' (1 Cor. 14:40)."[6] One of the weak points in church planting procedure has been inadequate accounting and reporting of financial matters. Many times church planters themselves do not know how to advise concerning financial bookkeeping. In chapter 4, regarding activity 11, I said that *from the beginning* financial contributions should be handled by the nucleus of believers and *not* by the team. At the very outset a treasurer and an assistant should be appointed from the nucleus to:

1. count all receipts, signing their names and the date on the tally sheet;
2. follow *simple* accounting procedure in keeping a financial

---

5. F. Jack Redford, *Planting New Churches* (Nashville: Broadman, 1978), 38. See also Melvin L. Hodges, *A Guide to Church Planting* (Chicago: Moody, 1973), 61–64, and Arthur S. Brown, *How One Church Can Start Another* (Chicago: Conservative Baptist Foreign Mission Society, 1957), 54–57.

6. Kilinski and Wofford, *Organization*, 199.

ledger which accounts for each receipt and expenditure by account number;

3. open a bank account in the name of the congregation and bank all funds as soon as possible after receipt, and
4. make all disbursements, except for petty cash, by check, signed by at least two people authorized by the congregation.

Kilinski and Wofford advise further that accounting should be simple and designed for the nonprofessional, "without unnecessary steps that might complicate the procedures. Accordingly, only basic records are recommended for church operations of small to medium size. . . . Simplicity in reporting accomplishes much more than an elaborate masterpiece."[7] One of the main reasons for encouraging an organizing congregation to manage its own finances from the beginning is to prepare it gradually for the day of organization, as well as to give it a reasonable base for further development during its progress toward adulthood.

Congregational Awareness of Financial Goals

Activity 35 (Goal: event 32): Regularly remind members of the financial goals of the church (figure 50).

Fig. 50
Regular Disciplined Giving

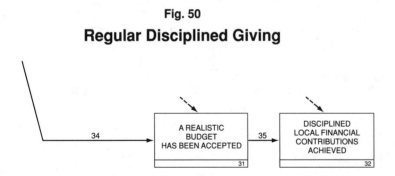

If we should agree with Kilinski and Wofford that "financial resources are significant as a tool in the fulfillment of the purposes and objectives of the church,"[8] then the entire membership of the body becomes vital in both the gathering of these resources and in the way they are used in the church's witness. There is entirely too much con-

---

7. Ibid. See also Charles L. Chaney and Ron S. Lewis, *Design for Church Growth* (Nashville: Broadman, 1977), 160.
8. Ibid., 197.

centration of power in the control of finances in the average local church. Again quoting Kilinski and Wofford,

> Some traditionalists may argue that the finances are the deacons' responsibility and must not be delegated; however, this is as erroneous as to say that the responsibility of the elders to feed the flock is limited only to them. It is obvious that while they oversee the ministry of teaching, others may and should share in this privilege, and so the deacons can and should allow others to have authority and responsibility for budgeting and expenditures under their overall direction.[9]

The old saying that "money talks" can be joined to another aphorism: "Those who control the purse strings have considerable power." Local church administration, when it comes to finances, must recognize this as a fact and head off the formation of any kind of power bloc. The treasurer is to be the *servant* of the brethren. The deacons, likewise, are certainly servants of the church.

Leading Christian workers throughout the world join me when I implore those with pastoral responsibility to keep their hands off the money! By taking this advice they will side-step possible criticism, suspicion, and temptation (1 Tim. 3:3; Titus 1:7, 11–12). Scandals caused by the financial impropriety of well-known television evangelists should warn church planters to avoid shoddy, secretive procedures in the handling of the Lord's money. *Transparent procedures in matters of financial accountability will actually encourage and accelerate giving.* It will build confidence in the church's administration. We must at all costs avoid being secretive about expenditures. *All* financial matters involving the expenditure of funds are of interest to the entire church membership. The church as a body *has a right to know how its money is used, and this on a regular, monthly basis.* Kilinski and Wofford say the objective of reporting is "to keep church members informed on financial matters and to encourage active participation in church affairs."[10] The treasurer should post a detailed monthly financial report showing both receipts and expenditures. This should be posted in such a way that all have easy access to it. During the "Pioneer Period" (see the complete PERT chart) the sponsoring body should also regularly receive a copy of this report so that their members likewise can be duly informed. In fact, this practice should continue as long as the church receives financial assistance from outside sources.

The annual budget of the church should be approved by the church at its annual meeting. This means that the financial goals for the coming year are understood and approved before going into effect.

9. Ibid., 197–98.
10. Ibid., 193.

Periodically, a public announcement can be made from the pulpit and progress or lack of progress reported.

Individual Financial Accounting

In order to encourage members to be systematic and regular in their financial stewardship, it is helpful to encourage giving by envelope. This has worked well in our experience. Each member may have a reusable envelope which is returned with the treasurer's receipt for the amount of the contribution. The envelope may be used over and over again. The treasurer keeps a ledger record of these contributions under the name of each contributor.

It should be stressed to all prospective members during their period of preparation that one of their spiritual responsibilities is to give faithfully. We have discussed how stewardship involves time, talents and gifts, and participation, but we should not be overly fearful to say forthrightly that it also means financially supporting the ministry of the church. In my judgment the failure of any church member to regularly contribute to the local church ministry for the Lord is the symptom of a serious *spiritual* problem, unless that person simply cannot do so. Stewardship is at the root of the matter. Often pastors are concerned about those who do not *tithe*. I feel, on the basis of what is taught in chapter 6, that this emphasis is superficial from the point-of-view of the New Testament. Tithers, too, can be spiritually ill in our churches. I am certain that many are. They tend to become smugly satisfied with themselves for giving 10 percent of their earnings to the Lord's work when they should be giving many times as much. Instead of "living it up" on the Lord's money, they should be heartily supporting those who are badly in need of support. Pastors should be teaching much more about carnal lifestyles and what the Word of God says concerning accountability. Someday we will all give account to the Lord of our stewardship of what is rightfully his (see chapter 6, activity 30).

Systematic Revision of Financial Goals

Activity 36 (Goal: event 33): Systematically revise the financial goals toward self-support (figure 51).

Fig. 51

Self-support Achieved

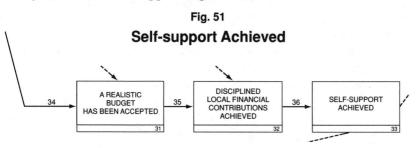

The implementation of activity 36 depends upon how the new church was planted. Some churches are planted without financial help from the outside. Those working in the *oikos* urban house church strategy, for instance, probably have started with little or no financial outlay. In such cases the church is practically self-supporting from the beginning. At least it has probably incurred no debts and is not receiving subsidies.

However, many times the sponsor of the new work continues over the course of a predetermined period to subsidize the salary of a full-time pastor. Also, the plan may expect repayment on a loan for the purchase of property or the construction of a building. In such cases, the church has a sizable debt, and the administration should sense a definite responsibility to reduce this debt and achieve self-support. The reason is simple if we keep in mind the long-range goal of our PERT strategy—maturity and the spontaneous planting of more new churches.

If such a church is being conscientiously guided in its growth toward the goal of reproduction and the planting of other churches, then it will consider self-support and financial independence to be of supreme importance. Rather than making all kinds of excuses for not reducing pastoral subsidy, and failing to make payments on loans previously agreed upon, the church will make a determined drive toward freeing itself from what I choose to call "baby clothes."

To do this, financial goals must be consistently revised upward toward self-support. Unnecessary purchases and expenditures for peripheral items or activities that are not fundamental to the ministry must be reduced to the bare minimum. A maximum of receipts must be channeled toward eliminating debt and achieving independence from outside funding. Incentive to do this can be maintained by regularly reminding the congregation of the long-range goals of the church. Such procedures will engender confidence in the administration. It will result in enthusiastic participation of more members.

There are three immediately recognizable benefits to achieving financial independence as soon as possible. First, the funds can be used by the sponsors to open other new churches. Second, self-support indicates organizational maturity and contributes to a new capacity for reproduction, apart from financial considerations. Third, a self-supporting church is autonomous and able to run its own affairs without coercion or interference from sponsors.

We have now considered four of the five goals that compose network III of our PERT plan. A church that takes care of itself must have reached all four. One important characteristic of such a church remains and will be presented in chapter 10. All of these goals are *interrelated* and *interdependent*. During what is called on the complete PERT chart the "Period of Growth and Organization," the new church must be wisely guided to progress simultaneously in each of the five subnetworks toward their goals. A consciousness of balance is the key to achieving goal or event 42.

10

Self-Identity

A mature church is capable of solving its own problems, and developing its own characteristic life style," according to C. Peter Wagner.[1] Such a church will take care of its own spiritual life as well as worship in a communicative, meaningful way. It will also be capable of responsible administration and management of its financial resources. There remains, however, one more important element in such a church. It will "take care of itself psychologically."[2]

Psychology is a social science that deals with the mind and mental processes, feelings, and desires. It seeks to study and order personal actions, traits, attitudes, and thoughts. We live in an age preoccupied with the in-depth study of psychology and its related disciplines. All manner of disorders are diagnosed and treated. Perhaps for some it will seem strange to insert psychology into our discussion of church planting, but the fact remains that it is not only individuals in society who desperately need to know who they are: Local church congregations also very much need to understand themselves.

How does a local church take care of itself psychologically? Allan Tippett called this the church's "self-image."[3] How does a church think about itself? How does it consciously define its own identity? In their

---

1. C. Peter Wagner, *Frontiers in Missionary Strategy* (Chicago: Moody, 1974), 164.
2. Ibid.
3. Allan R. Tippett, *Verdict Theology in Missionary Theory* (Lincoln, Ill.: Lincoln Christian College Press, 1969), 133, cited in Wagner, *Frontiers*, 164.

143

book about the responsible church, Peter Beyerhaus and Henry Lefever speak of "responsible selfhood."[4] This chapter proposes to briefly investigate the psychological state of the new church's lifestyle. This becomes very important as the new church grows and develops, especially in such countries as Portugal, Spain, Italy, Greece, or Austria where evangelical Christians are drastically outnumbered. How do evangelical churches think about themselves when they know that they number less than 1 percent of the national population?

The answer is obvious to one familiar with at least the European cultures. Evangelicals tend to have an inferiority complex. They are the underdogs. Their pastors are not recognized as having a profession. Believers are not accepted in society or regarded as having a valid religious belief. Many times they lose their jobs and are otherwise persecuted for their faith. For centuries lies about them and their faith have been widely believed. Under these conditions, no wonder that a certain pessimism grips many who despair of ever qualifying for any position of leadership in the community or nation.

This defeatist mindset to some degree characterizes churches around the world, but it must not be indulged in by a church expected to reproduce itself. Our goals for this part of our PERT plan and the activities required to reach them are certainly fundamental to a healthy self-image. Even though there are multitudes who are on "the broad way that leads to destruction," a local church that is expected to "think reproducible" must feel that it is an honor and a privilege to be among the few who are on "the narrow way that leads to life" (Matt. 7:13-14).

Stimulating Congregational Self-Determination

> *Activity 37 (Goal: event 34):* Practice procedures and use methods in the development of the lifestyle of the church that will lead to self-determination (figure 52).

Fig. 52
Independence from External Domination

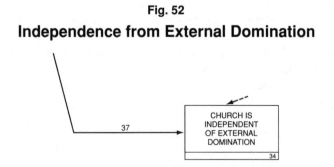

---

4. Peter Beyerhaus and Henry Lefever, *The Responsible Church and the Foreign Mission* (Grand Rapids: Eerdmans, 1964), 64, cited in Wagner, *Frontiers*, 164.

We all know that young children manifest the characteristics of their parents, especially the parent who spends the most time with them. Many times our attitudes toward other people, our racial prejudice, our phobias and complexes of various kinds can be traced directly to this source. Parents and guardians have an awesome responsibility.

I have emphasized repeatedly that in this "Period of Growth and Organization" all the elements in our plan for the new church must be kept in balance. In the church's internal life and affairs psychological development is of immense importance! The Scriptures clearly teach us that new believers can be compared to babies. Those who are truly born again need tender loving care just as any physical newborn. The church planting team and later the congregated church *inherit* the duty to give proper and adequate "parental care and guidance" to their spiritual offspring. Normally, every parent out in the world has this obligation. Invariably, our children are unconsciously influenced in their thinking processes by the way we think and express ourselves. This happens in a multitude of ways when we are not aware that it is taking place. It is an education without fanfare or ceremony. People are gradually, almost imperceptibly led to assume dogmatic attitudes, to feel strongly about certain people, and to act in certain ways in relation to their environment.

So also in the new church, whether in North America, Europe, Central America, or Africa. The aim for the church identified by Wagner is that it "harbors no inferiority complex which makes it suspect that it might be a tool of foreign influences. It is neither a dependent child nor a rebellious adolescent, having left such stages of development behind. It has developed a comfortable feeling of belonging within its cultural ecology, even when still a small minority. It does not feel it has to apologize to anyone for its existence."[5] Such a church has already attained a certain maturity. My concern in activity 37, however, is the course of its development to that point. The "stages of development" he mentions are crucial to attaining the goal.

Self-determination is the freedom to make up one's mind and act without outside influence. Given that God does and must control our church life, the proper sort of free will in view here is the right of a people to develop their own form of government and lifestyle, without coercion or undue outside influence. This healthy self-image includes a number of elements. Three are key, both personally and as a body. First, the new convert must be convinced clearly through Scripture of *great personal worth in God's sight*. This is basic to God's plan from before the foundation of the world (Eph. 1:4). Every believer must know that this preciousness to God is certain, without regard to race,

5. Wagner, *Frontiers*, 164.

social status, occupation, or level of education. "God so loved" this individual that he carried out his plan to save the person to live forever in God's blessing (John 3:16). Second, the individual has *personal responsibility to God*. Each believer must be made aware that God's command requires becoming a responsible, faithful steward of what has been committed to his or her management. This obviously means in practice that each believer, as a member of the new church, is to be taught this *personal relationship of responsibility to God*. The Christian has the privilege in this to make decisions that promote a personal walk with God (Gen. 5:24 and 6:9 and Gal. 5:25). *Personal* Bible study, *personal* prayer life, devotion, and communion with fellow believers are matters that involve the individual's will and self-determination. It is terribly wrong and harmful to the church as a body when members are pampered and so hindered from experiencing the development Wagner speaks about. To do away with childish things is essential in order to become a man (1 Cor. 13:11).

Third, each member has a *personal function in the body*. Every member must be free in the Holy Spirit to minister to and through this body. We discussed this in chapter 6 regarding activity 31 in connection with the gifts of the Holy Spirit. *Every* new Christian should be taught the Scriptures concerning gifts. Then *each one* should be guided in prayer and encouraged before God to personally sense responsibility regarding his function in body life. Each born-again member of the local church should be made conscious of his *important* place in the body (1 Pet. 4:10).

Only as the large majority of the members function in this manner can a local church achieve true self-determination. In many countries of Africa, Asia, and Europe, evangelical churches remain a small minority indeed. In every church, therefore, evangelical Christians need this healthy self-image, based on who they are in God's sight and their responsibilities to him and to fellow believers. Such a self-image is a great encouragement to carry on for God in a society where they are greatly outnumbered and underprivileged.

Event 34 in our PERT plan is, in a sense, the other side of the coin. When a church, in the person of its individual members, is practicing self-determination, it is essentially free from domination from the outside. It is also free from the unscriptural dictatorship of one or more individuals on the inside!

Attaining a Balanced Attitude of Independence

Activity 38 (Goal: event 35): Encourage and develop a scriptural attitude in the church with regard to independence (figure 53).

Fig. 53

Self-identity Established

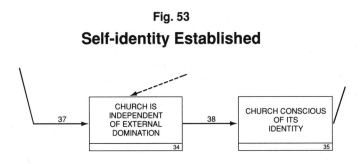

A balanced view of the local church's relationship with the larger church also affects the psychological wellbeing. The Bible provides such balance in developing a practical outworking of the doctrine of the church. The balance is between the consciousness of local *independence* on the one hand and that of *oneness* with all other Christians on the other.

One Church—Many Churches

There is no virtue in an exaggerated spirit of independence, either in our personal Christian experience or in relationships among churches. Of the one church, David J. Hesselgrave writes:

> It is patently clear that when our Lord said, "I will build my church" (Matt. 16:18), and when He prayed, "that they may all be one" (John 17:21), He had *one* Church in mind. It is tragically true that His builders tend to misconstrue and neglect this clear biblical teaching. Take, by way of example, the common interpretation of 1 Corinthians 3:16, "know ye not that ye are the temple of God, and that the Spirit of God dwelleth in you?" (KJV). Most Christians, without so much as a second thought, interpret this to mean that individual Christians are temples of God. Some do interpret the "temple of God" as a reference to the church at Corinth.[6]

Since the church that Christ is building is much bigger than the local assembly, we must help each new local church to recognize its identity with other Christian congregations, near and far. This takes determined effort. Churches can and should program interchurch activities, even with churches of another denomination. Even though regular participation and attendance is important in our own church, it is beneficial to us as members of Christ's body to fellowship occasionally with those brethren outside of our local fold. In my experience in mass evangelism in Portugal I found it to be an exhilarating experi-

---

6. David J. Hesselgrave, *Planting Churches Cross-Culturally: A Guide for Home and Foreign Missions* (Grand Rapids: Baker, 1980), 407–8. Emphasis Hesselgrave's.

ence for our local Christians. Their involvement in evangelism and counseling along with hundreds of others from dozens of other churches resulted in a visible injection of enthusiasm—a new realization of the greater dimension of the Church.

The Holy Spirit has one temple of God in mind in the New Testament which has its local manifestation in each local church. Speaking the same truth through Peter (1 Pet. 2:5–6), he portrays the church as a "spiritual house" of which Jesus Christ is the "precious corner *stone*" (v. 6), and to which individual believers, as "living stones" (v. 5), are being added.

Of the church as local congregations, Ernest De Witt Burton, in his commentary on Galatians, has an excellent short summary on *ekklesia* and its various usages—classical, Jewish, and Christian. He is convinced that the local sense of the word is undoubtedly the primary one in the New Testament. He favors the explanation that

> the use of the term in reference to the Christian church arose first on Gentile soil [although this is debatable] and with reference to the local congregations, but that the development of the ecumenical meaning was the easier because of the usage of קָהָל with reference to Israel as the covenant people of God, and the representation of this term in the LXX by ἐκκλησία.[7]

I make this very brief reference to the New Testament usage of *ekklesia* to reenforce the fact that there is *one church* of Jesus Christ even though it is organized geographically and denominationally into small local assemblies. D. W. B. Robinson offers valuable insight on the relationship between the one and the many:

> While there might be as many churches as there were cities or even households, yet the New Testament recognized only one *ekklesia* without finding it necessary to explain the relationship between the one and the many. The one was not an amalgamation or federation of the many. It was a "heavenly" reality belonging not to the form of this world but to the realm of resurrection glory where Christ is exalted (Eph. 1:20–23; Heb. 2:12; 12:23). Yet since the local *ekklesia* was gathered together in Christ's name and had Him in its midst (Matt. 18:20), it tasted the powers of the age to come and was the firstfruits of that eschatological *ekklesia*. So the individual local church was called "the church of God, which he hath purchased with his own blood" (Acts 20:28; cf. 1 Cor. 1:2; 5:2; 12:27).[8]

---

7. Ernest De Witt Burton, *A Critical and Exegetical Commentary on the Epistle to the Galatians* (Edinburgh: T. & T. Clark, 1921), 419.

8. D. W. B. Robinson, "Church" in *The New Bible Commentary* (1962 ed.). See also Karl Ludwig Schmidt, "ἐκκλησία," in Gerhard Kittel, ed., *Theological Dictionary of the New Testament*, 10 vols. (Grand Rapids: Eerdmans, 1965), 3:501–36. Schmidt also affirms

All who are familiar with the history of Christianity are aware of the historical reasons for today's divisions. Local church members today should be given sufficient instruction in this history to enable them to understand today's situation. Church planter Melvin Hodges writes summarily:

> In our day we do have an obstacle which the early church did not face. Today the Christian church is divided into denominations. The original church lost its purity and power and drifted into the Dark Ages. As there was a recovery of spiritual truth, the evangelicals broke away from the Roman Catholic Church. Then among the Protestants, as different Biblical truths were rediscovered, not all enjoyed the same degree of understanding, so that those receiving this light often found it necessary to separate from the parent body. Often this action was forced upon them. *It should be realized that many of the divisions that exist in the Protestant world today represent a struggle for truth.* While divisions in Protestantism are regrettable, yet, even this is to be preferred to the union in ignorance and error of the Middle Ages. Beyond the divisions of doctrine and organization, *the great majority of true Christians recognize their spiritual union with other people who have been born of the Spirit of God,* quite apart from their denominational affiliation.[9]

Today, we do not have a mother church in the sense that Jerusalem was in the first century. Our local churches are not related to any other church as many first century churches were related to the first church in Jerusalem. Rome would have us believe that we should be, nevertheless. The fact, however, is that our modern churches are true churches of Christ if they are ordered *only* by the Word of God, the Scriptures, in their faith and practice.

The catch with this statement is in the word *practice*. Much of what was actually "practiced" in the first century was not recorded in detail. There was also an evident development or evolution during the first century in matters related to organization and worship. These cannot help but have been strongly influenced by the local needs and cultural settings. This simply means that we must be extremely tolerant of one another in light of the fact that we do not know exactly what many of the details were in the practice of the different New Testament local churches. The Scriptures are silent about the order of worship, about how the Lord's Supper was celebrated, about the exact manner in

---

that "the sum of the individual congregations does not produce the total community or the Church." For support he points to 1 Cor. 1:2 and 2 Cor. 1:1 (506). He says further, "What counts is that the congregation [local] took itself to be representative of the whole Church" (535).

9. Melvin L. Hodges, *A Guide to Church Planting* (Chicago: Moody, 1973), 79–80. Emphasis author's.

which baptisms were performed, about how tithes and offerings were gathered, about whether the entire congregation voted on matters related to the assembly or whether the elders took this upon themselves in every instance. We do have some light from other literature of the late first century and beyond.

However, when we affirm in our day that the New Testament is our only rule of faith and practice, we are actually saying that we have no biblical right to demand conformity in matters about which the Scriptures maintain silence! If this were to be the order of the day, then many of the ungodly divisions that keep us aloof of one another would vanish into thin air. Our diverse practices would not hinder our warm fellowship in Christ our Head.

Interchurch Relationships

It is a biblical fact, then, that on the basis of a common adherence to the faith and practice of the Holy Scriptures we are obliged and privileged to enjoy Christian fellowship and spiritual communion with those of like precious faith, no matter what their denominational affiliation. Our union has already been consummated by the Holy Spirit himself (Eph. 4:3–6). What is our identity? We are members of one another, of Christ's body, which is far bigger than our local congregation, far larger than our local denominational affiliation, extending to the ends of the earth!

Many who have planted churches will readily agree with the list of benefits to the local church in avoiding isolation suggested by Hodges[10] and perhaps a few more might be added:

1. Cooperation affords a wider fellowship.
2. Cooperation facilitates mutual edification in the Christian life.
3. Cooperation often gives the local church a greater degree of stability in the things of the Lord.
4. Cooperation enables the churches to protect one another against false teachers, as well as against dangerous unscrupulous intruders or "wolves" (Acts 20:29).
5. Cooperation makes possible joint efforts in evangelism, education, benevolence, and the training of workers.

In this matter of interchurch relationships, Hesselgrave has some valuable planning counsel for churches and church planters on providing for two types of interchurch relationships: those with the sponsoring denomination or fellowship of churches and those with other Christian congregations.

10. Ibid., 80–81.

The kind of relationship which the local church will have with the sponsoring denomination will be determined by the leadership provided for the new church by the church-planter. It is vital, therefore, that the church-planter instruct the local leadership as to the nature of that relationship (as reflected in the founding document) and model the relationship in practice. . . .

If the local church is to avoid an unscriptural isolationism on the one hand and unscriptural forms of ecumenism on the other, both the basis and objectives of cooperation with other churches in the area should be prayerfully considered. A simple statement in the founding document or official record as to the essential items of the faith upon which cooperation and fellowship will be based will go far toward averting future dissention or confusion in the local church.[11]

Hesselgrave also relates the need for fellowship with other congregations through such activities as evangelistic efforts, worship services, special occasions and holidays, and community projects.[12]

This completes our review of PERT network III. Included in this plan, you will remember, are five main objectives (see figure 6) which together enable a church to "take care of itself":

1. Spiritual body life (chapter 6),
2. Contextualized worship services (chapter 7),
3. Adequate administration of church affairs (chapter 8),
4. Self-support in finances (chapter 9), and
5. Self-identity (chapter 10).

All five are "building blocks" that together form PERT event 42 (see complete chart). It is doubtful that a "mother church" will successfully plant a healthy, reproducing church unless its own example demonstrates these characteristics.

We will now turn our attention to network IV of our PERT plan to examine the question of the relationship of the new church to its surrounding culture.

11. Hesselgrave, *Planting Churches*, 419–20.
12. Ibid., 420.

11

A Relevant Message

Last in order of presentation but equal in priority to other goals of our PERT plan is the new church's surrounding culture. Chapter 5 (network II) dealt with evangelism and social concern (event 41). Network IV is concerned primarily with the cultural relevance of the message (event 43). Obviously, there is a close relationship between the two. C. Peter Wagner expresses well the burden of relevance:

> In almost all cases, relevancy seems to be a necessary counter-part to numerical growth. When a church is growing by conversions from the world, in some valid sense it must be relevant to the people it is appealing to. . . . A sealed off church, out of touch with those around it, lacks some very important element of maturity. Since it is God's purpose for the church to be an agent of reconciliation in the world, maturity implies dynamic fulfillment of that purpose. The message of reconciliation can only be communicated effectively if it is culturally relevant. Otherwise, it will win no one.[1]

How many church planters are oblivious to this? Church growth and cultural relevance are *not* mutually exclusive. Could this be one of the reasons why evangelical witness in many countries has made so little measurable headway during the past century or so? Church planters should ask themselves if they really understand the people. Louis J. Luzbetak wrote that "even centuries before the Science of

---

1. C. Peter Wagner, *Frontiers in Missionary Strategy* (Chicago: Moody, 1971), 167.

Culture was born, the most effective missionaries were those blessed with a deep appreciation of the diversity of cultures and of the important role which cultures play in human behavior."[2] Such "deep appreciation" can only be had as a result of genuine interest on our part. J. H. Bavinck goes right to the heart of the matter:

> Abstract, disembodied and history-less sinners do not exist; only very concrete sinners exist, whose sinful life is determined and characterized by all sorts of cultural and historical factors; by poverty, hunger, superstition, traditions, chronic illnesses, tribal morality, and thousands of other things. I must bring the gospel of God's grace in Jesus Christ to the whole man, in his concrete existence, in his everyday environment. It is obviously then a great error on my part if I do not take a person's culture and history seriously.[3]

What Is Culture?

Eugene A. Nida defines culture as "all learned behavior which is socially acquired, that is, the material and non-material traits which are passed on from one generation to another. They are both transmittable and accumulative, and they are cultural in the sense that they are transmitted by a society, not by genes."[4] Society is the vehicle of culture. Culture, therefore, is the way individuals of the society behave, think, react, and interact.[5] Over much of the world we also encounter, in Nida's terms, a *civilized* people with a very *heterogeneous* society composed of various *subcultures*: "There are often very distinct patterns of behavior for different regions, classes, or occupational groups, and a number of alternative patterns of behavior for individuals, even within the same subculture."[6]

What is the cultural context with which the church planter and the new church are faced? We begin to see the complexity of such a question through the eyes of Emil Brunner:

> The impulse to create the beautiful, to realize justice, to know the truth, to preserve the past, to enter into spiritual communication, to invent the new, to extend the range of interhuman communion to share the

2. Louis J. Luzbetak, *The Church and Cultures: An Applied Anthropology for the Religious Worker* (Pasadena, Calif.: William Carey Library, 1976), 3.

3. J. H. Bavinck, *An Introduction to the Science of Missions* (Philadelphia: Presbyterian & Reformed, 1961), 80, cited in Roy Joslin, *Urban Harvest* (Hertfordshire, England: Evangelical, 1982), 254–55.

4. Eugene A. Nida, *Customs and Cultures* (Pasadena, Calif.: William Carey Library, 1975), 28.

5. James P. Spradley, as an ethnographer, defines culture as "the acquired knowledge that people use to interpret experience and generate social behavior" (*The Ethnographic Interview* [New York: Holt, Rinehart and Winston, 1979], 5).

6. Nida, *Customs*, 30.

sufferings and joys of others; the impulse to submit the totality of life to ultimate directives and to give it meaning, unity and intelligibility, and finally to place everything under the divine will and receive it from the hands of God—all these are impulses out of which culture and civilization arise.[7]

Leslie A. White translates these varied impulses into a practical milieu, specifying that the cultural context "consists of tools, implements, utensils, clothing, ornaments, customs, institutions, beliefs, rituals, games, works of art, language, etc.,"[8] and Morris A. Inch theorizes that "culture reflects man's attempt to make the world a home to live in. It may take the form of a village hut or a great cathedral, but each represents alike the human saga."[9]

Local Cultural Characteristics

Due to the "heterogeneous" nature of society, importance should be given to *local* cultural distinctives. They vary considerably, even within a geographical area. Evangelical workers today are usually ready to admit the need for serious study of the culture as a preparation for fruitful evangelism and church planting.

Activity 39 (Goal: event 36): Carefully study how the people live in the area of the church (their cultural traits) (figure 54).

Fig. 54
Cognizance of Relevant Cultural Characteristics

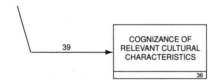

Ethnography

James P. Spradley claims that ethnography, the study of culture, has come of age. It began with field anthropology, but is no longer confined to "exotic cultures of far-off places." Rather, "it has become a fun-

7. Emil Brunner, *Christianity and Civilization*, vol. 2 (London: James Nisbet, 1974), 128, cited in Morris A. Inch, *The Evangelical Challenge* (Philadelphia: Westminster, 1978), 144.

8. Leslie A. White, *The Evolution of Culture* (Boston: McGraw-Hill, 1959), 3, cited in Inch, *Challenge*, 144.

9. Inch, *Challenge*, 145.

damental tool for understanding ourselves and the multicultural societies of the modern world."[10]

The church planter, whether foreign missionary or national, in today's complex society needs to understand how the people whom he is seeking to evangelize see their own experience. Spradley claims that ethnography offers

> a chance to step outside our narrow cultural backgrounds, to set aside our socially inherited ethnocentrism, if only for a brief period, and to apprehend the world from the viewpoint of other human beings who live by *different meaning systems.* . . . It is a pathway into understanding the cultural differences that make us what we are as human beings. . . . Cultural diversity is one of the great gifts bestowed upon the human species.[11]

Be that as it may, this "cultural diversity" presents a major problem for the church planter! He is obliged either to find or to personally do ethnographic studies of the target area. To personally research a community is a fascinating challenge and a radically new approach, far removed from the experience of the average missionary church planter! The odds are that he is not prepared for such a task.

I can here only introduce the "bare bones" of ethnographic procedure, hoping thereby to whet appetites for deeper study of the subject. Obviously, one needs adequate guidance by knowledgeable people in order to "do ethnography" if it is to have the maximum benefit for a church planting operation. It is being done for a myriad of other, less worthy causes; why not use it to accomplish the Lord's work? Spradley comes to our aid here with two companion texts that are extremely useful as tools for initiating the beginner in the task of doing ethnography.[12]

Spradley explains that ethnography is field work, the "disciplined study of what the world is like to people who have learned to see, hear, speak, think, and act in ways that are different."[13] The ethnographer learns about people *from the people. They* teach him. Assuming an attitude of almost complete ignorance, the student in this way "gets inside their heads."[14]

To do ethnography one must make what are called *cultural inferences* based on what people say, the way people act, and the artifacts or objects they use. Concentrating on inferences from what people say (the ethnographic interview), Spradley describes a strategy for getting

10. Spradley, *Interview*, iii.

11. Ibid., v. Emphasis author's.

12. *The Ethnographic Interview and Participant Observation* (New York: Holt, Rinehart and Winston, 1980).

13. Spradley, *Interview*, 3.

14. Ibid., 8.

Fig. 55

The Developmental Research Sequence

Major Tasks	Description of Tasks
1. Locating an Informant	Informant requirements: (1) thorough enculturation, (2) current involvement, (3) an unfamiliar cultural scene, (4) adequate time, (5) nonanalytic.
2. Interviewing an Informant	A series of friendly conversations into which three ethnographic elements are slowly introduced: explicit purpose, ethnographic explanations, and purpose.
3. Making an Ethnographic Record	Consists of field notes, tape recordings, pictures, artifacts, and anything else which documents the cultural scene under study.
4. Asking Descriptive Questions	The rapport process: apprehension, exploration, cooperation, participation. Descriptive questions aim to elicit a large sample of native utterances.
5. Analyzing Ethnographic Interviews	A distinct ethnographic analysis to help to discover what things mean to the informant and what future questions to ask to further clarify meaning.
6. Making a Domain Analysis	A domain is a symbolic category that includes other such categories. Domain analysis leads to finding other kinds of domains through structural questions.
7. Asking Structural Questions	Five major types: verification questions, cover term questions, included term questions, substitution frame questions, and card sorting structural questions.
8. Making Taxonomic Analysis	This involves a search for the internal structure of domains and leads to identifying contrast sets (considered in step 9).
9. Asking Contrast Questions	The meaning of a symbol can be discovered both by finding out how it is similar and how it is different from other symbols. Seven types of contrast questions.
10. Making a Componential Analysis	The entire process of searching for contrasts, sorting them out, grouping some together as dimensions of contrast, and entering all information in a paradigm.
11. Discovering Cultural Themes	Make cultural inventory; list unidentified domains; collect sketch maps; list examples; make diagram of scene; write summary overview.
12. Writing an Ethnography	Involves skillfully written communication findings; necessarily will be partial, incomplete, and need revision.

Adapted from James P. Spradley, *The Ethnographic Interview* (New York: Holt, Rinehart and Winston, 1979).

people to talk about what *they* know, using their own verbal symbols. He calls this "The Developmental Research Sequence." It is a series of twelve major tasks, activities, or steps (see figure 55).

In *Participant Observation*, Spradley provides a simple graphic display of "The Ethnographic Research Cycle," showing in a kind of cyclical pattern the principal ethnographic tasks from the selection of the ethnographic project to the writing of an ethnography.[15]

I believe that this ethnographic approach to our PERT activity 39 should produce a significant breakthrough toward understanding the inner workings of any local cultural scene, large or small. Anyone putting this into practice in a given cultural scene could eventually produce a very down-to-earth manual, adapting Spradley's twelve steps to specifically meet the requirements of the church planter and the new churches working with the people studied.

It will soon become evident, as professional ethnographers have discovered, that the study of any way of life or cultural scene must be limited in some way.[16] The church planter doing ethnographic surface and in-depth analysis should work to identify specific categories of thought—what Spradley calls *cultural domains*—and limit investigation to these areas. The sort of ethnographic project a church planting team or a local church would face must be carefully chosen. Spradley refers to the "scope" of the investigation. The scope of research can range from *macro-ethnography* to *micro-ethnography*. Macro-ethnography requires years of research by a number of workers. Micro-ethnography takes less time and effort.[17] Spradley's book, *Participant Observation*, concentrates on the practical micro-ethnography project. This undoubtedly is what the church planter is interested in.[18]

Ethnographic research is a tool that merits serious consideration in many cross-cultural church planting situations. If we continue to neglect doing this type of study, we will be less fruitful in evangelism and church planting. The cause of evangelism and church planting desperately needs a *workable* way to correctly understand local culture.

Activity 40 (Goal: event 37): Study how to adapt biblical theology and the life of the new church to the local cultural scene (figure 56).

How can biblical theology and the New Testament church it builds be related and relevant to its indigenous culture? The situation I best know is that of Portugal, so perhaps we can use both the Roman Catholic and the Protestant experiences there to discern some ideas. Informed Roman Catholics, including the Pope, became aware of the urgent need for relatedness and relevance from Vatican Council II. It did not become a primary concern of Portugal's Catholics until 1974,

15. Spradley, *Participant*, 29
16. Spradley, *Interview*, 132.
17. Spradley, *Participant*, 30.
18. Ibid.

Fig. 56

Cultural Adaptation Achieved

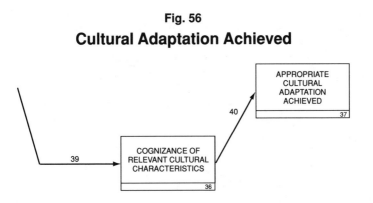

when concerted communistic activity challenged conservative Romanism. How relevant was the faith, after all? Most Portuguese have never known anything but a superstitious, paganized, idolatrous form of Roman Christianity. Numerous shrines perpetuated a strong mariolatry (the cult of the Virgin Mary). Even John Paul II, himself a devotee of Mary, made a special pilgrimage to Portugal to the shrine of Fatima in May of 1982 to thank the virgin for saving his life from the assassin's bullet. Further, Portugal's 20 percent rate of illiteracy is the highest in western Europe. If Roman Catholicism faced a crisis of relevancy in this kind of situation, how should we as evangelicals proceed? Once PERT event 36 has been realized the church should understand more about the cultural characteristics that explain the observable phenomena. There is a need and an answer—the gospel.

Contextualization

Contextualization seeks to translate the absolutes of the Scriptures so that they take into account changing language and differing ideas among cultures. The idea is not to change the gospel but to enable it to speak with relevance to the needs of people with whom we are working. Those needs continually change and may be only partly understood.[19] George W. Peters suggests several principles to help translate God's truth into meaningful terms through contextualization.[20] The first principle is absolute condemnation of certain aspects of the culture and separation from them. Scripture simply will not tolerate certain things. Light has no fellowship with darkness (2 Cor. 6:14). Reference has already been made to a questionnaire sent out to church planters in Portugal from eight different evangelical groups. One question was:

19. James O. Buswell, II, "Contextualization: Theory, Tradition and Method," in David J. Hesselgrave, ed., *Theology and Mission: Papers Given at Trinity Consultation No. 1* (Grand Rapids: Baker, 1978), 87.
20. Trinity Evangelical Divinity School, DMS 211, class notes, July 1982.

Fig. 57

Portuguese Cultural Characteristics Condemned by Scripture

Religious Traditions	Moral Deficiencies	Society in General
1. Idolatrous religious festivals	1. Egoism	1. Bull fights
2. Religious fanaticism	2. Decay of moral standards in the home	2. Exaggerated pride of history
3. Religious superstition	3. Obscene language	3. The "cult" of sports events and the beach
4. Mixture of religious faith and politics	4. Counter-culture promoted by TV	4. Atheistic ideology
5. Mariolatry, the cult of the Virgin Mary	5. Hypocrisy	5. Lack of discipline
6. Patron saints and the cult of the saints	6. Dishonesty, lying	6. Insubordination
7. Worship of images, possession of images	7. Lack of sincerity	7. Civil disobedience
8. Religious pilgrimages	8. Lack of moral character and personal integrity	8. Lack of respect for authority of any kind
9. Religious ignorance	9. Concubinage, fornication	9. Materialistic teaching in the schools, humanism
10. Religious persecution	10. Practice of abortion	10. Popular traditions of pagan origin
11. Religious practice separated from the Word of God	11. Alcoholism, use of tobacco and other health hazards	11. Leaving life to chance, let come what may, what God wills, hopefully it will be all right
12. Spiritism	12. The "New Morality"	
13. Witchcraft	13. Gossip—intrigue	
14. Religious indifference	14. Negligence—carelessness	
15. Heretical sects—Jehovah's Witnesses and Mormons	15. Failure to keep one's word	
	16. Deceitfulness—fraud	
	17. Public lotteries	
	18. Materialism	
	19. Greed	
	20. Cruelty to less fortunate	
	21. Male chauvinism, wife beating	

Samuel D. Faircloth, "Planting New Churches in Portugal" (Questionnaire responses, Nov. 1983).

> As you reflect on the Portuguese culture and the life-style of people among whom you work, which characteristics do you consider to be *acceptable* in the light of Scripture and which to be *condemned* by Scripture?[21]

Characteristics they listed as condemned by Scripture can be formed into three categories, as in the chart of figure 57. Marital unfaithfulness is almost traditional. Lying is a way of life. Disobedience to the civil law is commonplace. Exploitation of the poor, cruelty to the less fortunate, general dishonesty, wife-beating, alcoholism and male chauvinism—all such are condemned as sinful practices by clear teaching of the Scriptures. Consequently, they must be condemned by the church planter and the new church.[22] But how should they go about it?

The second principle warns us that many times such condemnable practices must be patiently tolerated until the person's own conscience has been built up to recognize them as sin and thus to condemn them personally. This is a process of conscientization. In the case of the new convert, the church planter and later the local church must patiently teach specific biblical truth so that the new convert's Christian conscience may be gradually informed by the Word of God through the ministry of the Holy Spirit. It should not be formed by the opinions or personal views of the church planter. There are hundreds of specifics concerning the Christian life in the New Testament (for example, Col. 3:1–4:1). Along with the teaching of specifics, a Christian conscience is nurtured in a new convert by observing a consistent Christian life in those who profess to be Christians, including the evangelist (1 Tim. 4:16).

A third principle in evaluating a cultural element with a view to contextualization of Christian truth is the intention to convert secular concepts by giving them Christian meaning. The word "saint" to the twentieth century Portuguese refers to a mystical spiritual elite. However, the Bible clearly teaches that all believers in Christ are to be called saints (such as Rom. 1:7; 2 Cor. 1:1; 6:1–6; 13:13; Eph. 1:1; Phil. 1:1; 4:21–22). In the context of Romanism, many valid biblical terms commonly used by people must be reinterpreted to restore their original biblical meanings.

The fourth way in which to react to cultural practices is obviously to adapt to them or to freely adopt them. In response to the above mentioned questionnaire, workers also listed acceptable cultural characteristics in the light of Scripture (see figure 58). As Latins, for instance,

21. Samuel D. Faircloth, "Planting New Churches in Portugal" (photocopied questionnaire, Nov. 1983), 6.
22. Luzbetak, *The Church*, 183. He calls this "cultural surgery" (Rom. 11:19, 24; Col. 3:9–10; Matt. 5:29–30): "Compromise is impossible when 'surgery' happens to be the only means of saving the true and full meaning of the Gospel."

Fig. 58

Portuguese Cultural Characteristics Supported by Scripture

Religious or Spiritual Qualities	Moral Qualities
1. Fear of God—elementary religious education	1. Family care for the elderly
2. General belief in the Trinity	2. Catholic social programs (wide variety)
3. Belief in the Ten Commandments	3. Solidarity among those who suffer
4. General love of God	4. Hard work (true of many)
5. Respect for the Bible	5. Friendliness, temperament open to others
6. Belief in God's existence	6. Simplicity
7. Religious bent or tendency of sensibility	7. Readiness to help a neighbor or stranger
8. Traditional respect for the church	8. Sympathetic, warm hearted
9. Sincere seeking for God by many	9. Cautious, prudent with outsiders
10. Religious devotion	10. Simple confidence in others
11. Admission of sin	11. Sacrificial service when engaged in something they believe in
12. Interest in the person of Christ	12. Hospitality
	13. Generally a humble people
	14. Open to conversation
	15. Generous
	16. Likable
	17. Affectionate

Samuel D. Faircloth, "Planting New Churches in Portugal" (Questionnaire responses, Nov. 1983).

the Portuguese are warm, affectionate people. It is common practice to greet one another with a kiss on both cheeks, especially among youth and between adults and children. A parting handshake is normal. A "bear-hug" is expected between friends. Speaking with gestures is common. Emotions are seldom hidden. For this reason contextualization of the messenger helps to contextualize the message. In such a context, the messenger must demonstrate the warmth of the gospel by his personal adaptation to these cultural traits. It is essential in order that evangelism be successful.

A fifth principle important to the evaluation of a cultural practice involves substitution. In the case of the application of the first principle, where it has been necessary to condemn and eliminate a certain cultural trait, it is imperative that an acceptable substitute be found to put in its place. Social gatherings that center their attention on detrimental, un-Christian activities must be replaced by worthy Christian social events capable of promoting real New Testament *koinonia*.[23] Latin people want and need such fellowship frequently, apart from regular worship services and the routine activities of the local church.

Activity 41 (Goal: event 38): Program the church life-style to match the acceptable cultural characteristics (figure 59).

Fig. 59

Church Adapted to Environment

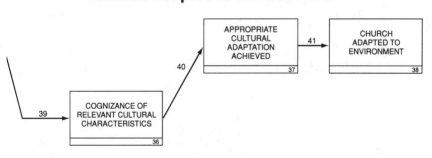

Having made a serious effort to understand the local culture (PERT activities 39 and 40) using some form of ethnographic research and giving attention to the foregoing principles of contextualization focused by Peters, the local church can better proceed to program its

23. Ibid., 180–81. Luzbetak, in speaking of the linkages between new Christian ways and the existing cultural structure, insists that severed linkages must be replaced with new ones which can come from the Christian message or some other innovation. "Severed functions must never be ignored, otherwise the corresponding needs will be filled by some other non-Christian (usually traditional) way." He claims that "syncretism is an evident sign that the missionaries have not succeeded in filling felt needs."

approach to the community, confident of the relevance of its actions. In its goal to "live for others" (event 41, chapter 5), New Testament evangelism and significant resultant social concern can make practical contact with the "world." Therefore, activity 41 is a follow-through based on cultural understanding. It aims to "position" the church for effective ministry to the community.

Communicating the Gospel to Non-Christians

Remember that we must here present networks II, III, and IV one at a time, but they are not achieved or reached in this fashion. During this extended period of growth and organization all three networks will be in simultaneous motion, with efforts moving in the direction of all nine goals (events 15, 18, 21, 26, 30, 33, 35, 38, and 40). Progress in each case will vary according to the circumstances.

> *Activity 42 (Goal: event 39):* Study how better to present the gospel in light of the findings (figure 60).

Fig. 60

Contextualized Evangelistic Message

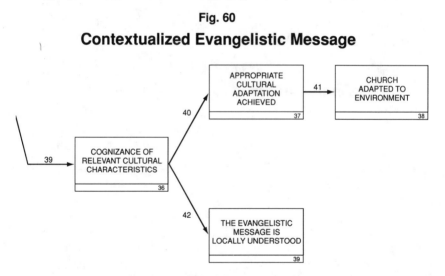

Contextualized Evangelism

The goal of evangelism in network II can only be realized by means of a clear presentation of the gospel which has been contextualized to be relevant to the culture of the non-Christian. The goal of a culturally relevant evangelism is to see conversions from the world. "The gospel becomes meaningful [to the world] . . . only as it is contextualized."[24]

24. David J. Hesselgrave, *Planting Churches Cross-Culturally: A Guide for Home and Foreign Missions* (Grand Rapids: Baker, 1980), 209.

Bruce Nicholls spoke clearly of this in Lausanne in 1974, proposing this definition and exposition of the concept:

> Contextualization means the translation of the unchanging content of the Gospel of the kingdom into verbal form meaningful to peoples in their separate cultures and within their particular existential situations. In this regard it is reaffirmed that this Gospel of the kingdom as defined in Holy Scripture is *totally relevant* to man in the totality of his need. This follows because the Gospel was designed and provided by the same God who made the human heart and who knows the depth of man's alienation from Him and from his fellows. All who do the work of the evangelist are under solemn obligation to *guard* this relevant, revealed Gospel. The task in evangelism is to communicate the Gospel to all men in terms meaningful to their cultural identity and existential condition. The *problem* in contextualization as popularly understood is that one can all too easily drift into an unwarranted and God-displeasing syncretism. By this is meant the sort of accommodation to the cultural values of a people that results in a mixture of biblical truth and ethnic religion. Syncretism invariably and inevitably dilutes and distorts the fact that Jesus Christ alone is Lord and Savior. Furthermore, when one attempts to translate biblical truth into the language and culture of a people, one is under solemn obligation to produce what will be no more and no less than the normative Word of God. The more one reflects on the task of contextualization, the more conscious one becomes of the larger task, of seeking to structure theological thought within each separate culture in such a way that the total corpus of biblical truth is more faithfully communicated to every man in his own culture.[25]

Hesselgrave further comments that "the supracultural truth of Christ becomes meaningful within any cultural system as it takes on the various forms of that system: linguistic, personal, social, and ecclesiastical."[26]

Caution in Contextualization

Norman R. Ericson, in his helpful discussion about the implications related to contextualization, establishes four categories for determining how far contextualization can go. A summary of this list and the limits in each category are:

1. *The core*: revelation and salvation in Jesus Christ. Contextualization is only possible to the extent that cultural and biblical concepts may be compared.

25. Bruce Nicholls, "Theological Education and Evangelization," in J. D. Douglas, ed., *Let the Earth Hear His Voice* (Minneapolis: World Wide, 1975), 647. Emphasis Nicholls's.
26. David J. Hesselgrave, *Communicating Christ Cross-Culturally: An Introduction to Missionary Communication* (Grand Rapids: Zondervan, 1978), 84.

2. *The substance*: the gospel tradition in apostolic transmission. Contextualization may extend only so far as a contemporary culture may be compared with its biblical equivalents.
3. *The application*: exhortations addressed to particular people. Entire contextualization of applications is possible insofar as personal qualities and Christian virtues remain universal.
4. *The expression*: quality of life as a cultural setting. Universal Christian virtues must be expressed appropriately for a culture. Contextualized expression must deliver the message in meaningful, culture-relevant behavior.[27]

The obvious cultural caution here is that God's inspired inscripturated truth not be lost or adulterated as the evangelist attempts to be culturally relevant. The integrity of the Bible's text and concepts is vitally important!

Activity 43 (Goal: event 40): Evangelize with these culturally relevant considerations in mind (figure 61).

Fig. 61

Conversions from the World

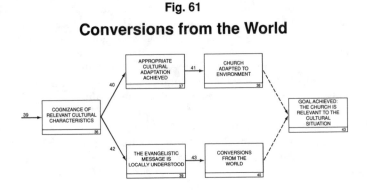

Peters has suggested five pertinent considerations for authentically contextualizing the Christian message: (1) conceptualization; (2) configuration; (3) exposition; (4) implications, and (5) confrontation.[28]

Conceptualization

We are privileged in the English speaking world to have a number of modern translations and paraphrases of the Scriptures. Every translation of the original languages is something of a paraphrase. God accommodated himself to the human language of biblical authors. In so doing

27. Norman R. Ericson, "Implications from the New Testament for Contextualization," in Hesselgrave, *Theology and Mission*, 83.
28. Trinity Evangelical Divinity School, DMS 211, class notes, July 1982.

he communicated within the vocabulary of these forty or so men, which must be communicated in words and grammatical constructs that convey to our minds the same conceptual content. Charles H. Kraft calls these analogous forms "dynamic equivalents."[29] Since in church planting one of the first jobs is one-to-one evangelism, the missionary must make sure he is understood. In so doing, however, he must take care that the biblical message is not distorted. Kraft maintains that biblical *language form* may have to be changed in order to preserve the content of the message. He says, "It is the message of the Bible that is sacred, not the languages themselves." In a day in which the text of Scripture is under attack from within the church, and *inerrancy* has to be defined even among so-called evangelicals, Kraft has raised suspicions. One can well ask whether plenary verbal inspiration of the Bible is in jeopardy if Kraft's free-phrasing principles are accepted.[30] Caution is a mild word when we are dealing with this subject.

We can affirm Kraft's point that the biblical writers "expect to be understood." We, too, want to be understood as we seek to reach men with the good news. Our language, our choice of words in a language must convey what the original author intended. Extreme care must be exercised so that the decoded message is as much like the original as possible. Luzbetak, Kraft, Peters, and others correctly emphasize the importance of rapport between the missionary church planter and the potential convert. A basic respect for the people, mutual admiration, and friendship are essential to "speaking their language" in our ministry.

Configuration

Configuration is the shaping of the message in such a way that it moves hearers to do want God wants. Of course, we must remember here that the Holy Spirit was not only the divine Author of the Scriptures; he also has the unique ministry of applying them to human hearts (John 16:8–11, 13–15). I, as his servant, must walk in the Spirit in order to allow him his part in the configuration of the message to the mind and heart of the person to whom I am witnessing. For instance, the Portuguese love drama; they also love poetry and the narration of stories. A Portuguese audience is moved by a dramatic story such as the "soaps" on television. They easily identify with stories that approximate their own cultural experience. In this sense they are like

29. Charles H. Kraft, *Christianity in Culture: A Study in Dynamic Biblical Theologizing in Cross-Cultural Perspective* (Maryknoll, N.Y.: Orbis, 1979), 272–75.
30. For further valuable comment on Kraft's controversial position, see the significant recent work of David J. Hesselgrave and Edward Rommen, *Contextualization: Meanings, Methods, and Models* (Grand Rapids: Baker, 1989), 59–69. Also, Edward N. Gross published an in-depth analysis of Kraft in *Is Charles Kraft an Evangelical? A Critique of "Christianity in Culture"* (Collingswood, N.J.: Christian Beacon, 1985).

the audiences of Jesus in the Gospels. Biblical narration is of interest to them. This certainly is one key to their hearts—a human story which transmits the message.

Exposition

People listen with rapt attention to anyone who can effectively expound the Word of God. There is no substitute for careful historical-grammatical hermeneutics. Likewise, there is no substitute for thoughtful, honest exegesis of the biblical text that keeps the language of the audience in mind; that seeks to expound for the listener what Moses, Isaiah, Matthew, or Paul were inspired to record. I have found it to be a great thrill to be able to communicate God's message in the local language to hungry hearts from every strata of society, to be a fellow-laborer with Paul, Peter, and John. Their words were warm, feeling words, filled with God's love and tender compassion for the lost. Exposition must express this as did Paul in Romans 9, Philippians 1, and Ephesians 1. Where there is doubt about meaning, humility and a spirit of fairness and objectivity must prevail.

Implications

Certainly, Scriptural truth at any point carries ethical implications. Herein lies the failure of much of our preaching and teaching at home and abroad. Our God demands obedience. Throughout biblical history blessing is with the obedient. How Israel suffers even to this day in her disobedience. Peters asks, "Why does our theology slip so easily into rationalism?"[31] The answer would appear to be in the fact that ethics have been conveniently forgotten, perhaps for a multitude of reasons! The implications of the very name *Lord Jesus Christ* are enough to shame most of us and bring us to our knees, if we take it seriously. Woe to the missionary or church planter who knows but does not obey in his biblical exposition.

Confrontation

Anyone who will seek to plant a church, whether in the city or out in the provinces away from the larger urban centers, will confront Satan in a stronghold. He is called "your adversary" (1 Pet. 5:8), and he is, oh, so real! Witchcraft, demonism, and idolatry hold people in their grip, even though the census might declare them to be Christian. Since my background is the Roman Catholic setting I can diagnose Roman Catholicism as syncretistic, for example. In such countries as Poland, mariolatry abounds, as does the cult of the saints in general. Alliances

31. Trinity Evangelical Divinity School, DMS 211, class notes, July 1982.

with pre-Christian pagan customs and feasts are everywhere evident. Preaching the biblical Christian message to these people obliges the missionary to fearlessly confront the enemy and to proclaim the truth as did Paul to the Romans and the Galatians.

The contextualization of Christian theology in church planting anywhere in the world is essentially a careful communication of the biblical faith in the language of the people, interpreted in relation to their specific problems in a given situation. As has been pointed out, the missionary must also contextualize himself as a living example of the doctrine.

In fully realizing the goals of PERT events 38 and 40 a new church has also achieved one of the last of the three main requirements for the church to be mature, able, and motivated to reproduce itself: namely (in event 43) it is relevant to the cultural situation.

In the last chapter I will recapitulate what has been presented, emphasizing salient factors fundamental to actual reproduction.

The Period of Reproduction

12

Motivation and Capacity for Reproduction

Expected Results

The Period of Reproduction in our PERT plan should result when the goals of the previous periods are being more-or-less faithfully achieved. When a local church actively reproduces itself by planting other new churches, we can be certain that it somehow has been prepared previously.

Churches which are reproducing themselves and planting other new churches continue to need revisions in their local organization. They continue to grow spiritually and numerically. This means that churches that reach maturity have not "arrived." Constant attention must be given to the status of each of the networks of our PERT plan. This is precisely the great advantage of having a plan! A church that has a plan can ask itself the important questions as a check on its state of health. Is evangelism a priority of our congregation? Do we have a world vision as well as a local vision for the salvation of the lost? Are we doing what we can for the social needs of the people we are seeking to reach as well as the community itself? How is the church functioning in worship? Are administrative needs being met? Is the church functioning as a body? Are our members faithful to their financial responsibilities? Does the church have a healthy self-image? Do we continue to be in tune with the cultural surroundings so we can be heard by the unsaved?

The basic idea is to "keep in training." The reason is simple: Living things change; the local church is a living thing. Members enter and leave for one reason or another. The leadership has a solemn responsibility to understand this and to keep itself and the church on its toes. The Holy Spirit does not sleep. He has plans and we should keep in top shape for his use. When we allow ourselves to be occupied with other interests and pursuits he cannot fill us and send us forth to fulfil the Great Commission. We are living in a world in which otherwise keen Christians are all tied up in lifestyles which have nothing whatsoever to do with the purposes of God! *Members of a mature, adult church must avoid worldly pursuits like the plague.* Satan is ever so subtle, so be alert to the temptation to veer off into paths that rob the body of its motivation to reproduce. We can be certain that when the Spirit has the preeminence in our daily lifestyle we will not find ourselves involved in activities that divert us from spiritual reproduction.

Unfortunately, motivation is lacking in the majority of churches. It is a sad fact that most local churches around the world, and especially in the West, have no vision whatsoever to become immediately involved in starting new churches. Therefore, at the close of the twentieth century we are obliged to conclude that to reproduce and to possess the capacity to do so is by no means automatic or characteristic of today's evangelical churches. We need to make a practice of giving serious attention to obedience—obedience to God's inspired Word. Through this channel the Spirit will renew motivation and revive spiritual life in the church.

Parachurch Evangelism

Challenge

Throughout the world today, churches are being challenged in a random manner to participate in a rather wide variety of evangelistic thrusts into the spiritual darkness of society. Well-meaning parachurch organizations multiply, even in countries with an extremely low percentage of believers. Almost every one of these organizations is missionary in spirit, inspired, and supported by foreign entities. In most cases the burden is evangelistic. The simple gospel is communicated. Sooner or later, however, the conservation of spiritual fruit becomes a burden, a preoccupation, and even a frustration for them. The reason is understandable. As a rule parachurch organizations are not constituted for consistent spiritual nurture. I was approached while working in Portugal by a good brother in Christ who had been made supervisor of evangelism in a large parachurch organization there. He told me that he was firmly reminded by the director that he must *not* think in terms of new churches, for: "Our organization does not found new churches." And yet they are evangelizing hundreds of people! Where are these converts to go? They reply: "To the nearest church; the nearest church should be challenged to take the people in." The nearest church could be many miles away. And what if there is no desire by this church to cooperate? What then?

Reflections

Several observations are in order as we reflect on this situation. First, in most cases the nearest local church, mission, or preaching point is *totally unprepared* to care for dozens of new "babies." It was not their decision to have a family. They have little practical vision for discipling people outside their folds. Second, clear New Testament precedents seem to demonstrate that the local churches were moved by the Spirit into evangelistic witness that resulted, not only in converts, but also in new congregations which, in turn, repeated the process (Jerusalem, Antioch, Ephesus, Philippi, and Thessalonica). The churches of the first century were spiritually alive. Evangelism came from within the church; it was not randomly imposed from without. Third, it is unscriptural as well as deplorably neglectful to leave new converts without adequate spiritual nurture and care. The apostles cared for new Christians by planting and ministering to fellowships— new local bodies of converts duly constituted (Acts 14:23; 15:36, and 18:23; 1 Cor. 1:2; Gal. 1:2; Phil. 1:1; 1 Thess. 1:1; Titus 1:5, and Philem. 2). The apostles did not plant Bible study groups; they planted churches!

This is precisely what is needed all over the world today. Biblical records of early missionary activity, as well as early postapostolic history of the church, teach us that the will of the Holy Spirit is the continuous planting of new churches throughout the world.

It is my purpose in this last chapter to recapitulate fundamental prerequisites to effective reproduction in church planting. Just what is involved in the life of any church that imparts the motivation and the capacity to plant new churches?

Steps to Maturity: Networks I Through IV

Figure 62 is a review of the principal elements of our PERT plan, without the numbering used throughout the text. These objectives are concrete steps in a logical plan of action in which each event contributes to desired results. It will help to focus both partial and total goals of church planting.

Fig. 62

Steps to Maturity

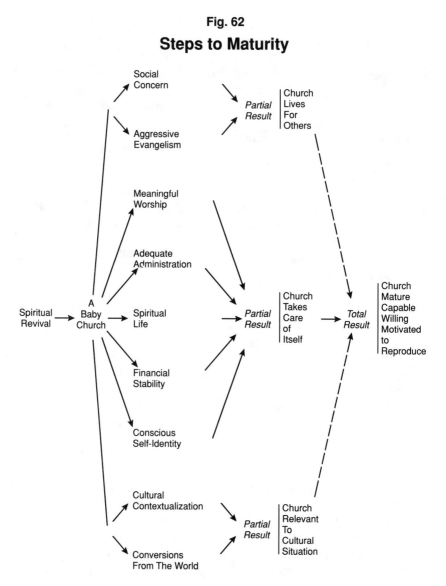

Step One—Make Necessary Preparations

Spiritual revival is fundamental to evangelism and church planting, as was noted in chapter 3. The world has crept into many churches. Even full-time Christian workers and missionaries fall victims to attitudes that characterize what the Scriptures call the "old man" and the "flesh." The carnality that Paul opposed so forcefully in the Corinthian church must be faced head-on in our evangelical churches. There reigns a selfishness and egotism, even in the ministry, which Scripture roundly condemns.

Those who would effectively evangelize must "walk by the Spirit" (Gal. 5:16). Spiritual cleansing and renewal of the local church will clear the way for obedience. As people get back into close fellowship with the Lord and with one another the church will grow. The Holy Spirit will be free to accomplish his unique ministry among lost men and women. "The lust of the flesh and the lust of the eyes and the boastful pride of life" (1 John 2:16) will fade and a love for God will take its place. Church planting is a spiritual battle. The enemy of our souls is entrenched in his strongholds. The battle will be won "'not by might nor by power, but by My Spirit' says the LORD of hosts" (Zech. 4:6). Therefore, those who would engage in church planting must especially heed the admonition of Ephesians 5:18 to be filled with the Spirit.

Step Two—Plant a "Baby" Church

In order to accomplish this goal, a number of matters must have our attention:

The team
Paul and others did not work alone. Jesus sent out his disciples two by two. It appears in Scripture that the Lord would have us work together in planting churches. It is wise to carefully and prayerfully select a team to be directly responsible for a new effort at church planting.

The target area
The Spirit will give wisdom as to the area to study and the survey method to use. He will also help in the preparation and methods for evangelism.

Initial evangelism
The Spirit will also lead as evangelism begins. Prayer will be so important. Those engaged in church planting are servants of the Lord. We must follow *his* leading as initial contacts are made. Clear, contextualized communication is a must. Careful attention should be paid to James F. Engel's "Spiritual-Decision Process" shown in figure 18 (p. 66).

The nucleus
New believers should be introduced to one another. The nucleus of believers will grow as evangelism continues. Homes will become meeting places as in New Testament times. Since evangelism is intimately related to making disciples, new converts should become disciples— learners and servants of the Lord. Discipling is extremely important because our goal is reproducing Christians. Such Christians make reproducing congregations. We should take this process very seriously,

especially during the beginning stages, if we are to "think and act reproducible." Reproduction must be built into the foundation of a new work. Such discipling also prepares the convert for public symbolic confession of his faith through water baptism.

Formal organization

As congregational consciousness develops in the growing nucleus and believers become aware of what membership in a local church fellowship will mean for them, plans should be made to formally organize the group into a local church. Exact requirements and procedures will depend upon the denomination or affiliation of the sponsoring or "mother" church.

Denomination

This book, though undenominational in its general approach, is definitely congregational rather than episcopal or presbyterial in the form of government advocated. This is more typical among evangelicals.

Step Three—Learn to Live for Others

As the young church continues to grow, I have recommended that it keep three partial objectives constantly in mind, events 41, 42, and 43 on the PERT chart, or in unnumbered form in figure 62 (p. 176). The reader has become aware that the three must be planned in harmony with one another, and wise leaders will try to make constant progress toward all three as interdependent facets.

Evangelism

One of the partial results to be sought in working toward maturity in a church is that it *live for others*. It must become a missionary church. It must not be turned in on itself. Rather, it must see "the fields that they are white for harvest" (John 4:35b). A mature church has the compassion of the Lord for the lost.

Social concern

Chapter 5 demonstrated that, although this compassion and burden for the souls of men is of primary importance, many times it is necessarily concerned as well with physical needs. Evangelism takes place in a physical environment which the evangelist cannot ignore and does not wish to ignore. Therefore, in living for others, the church will evangelize the lost and show "bridges of love" in helping to meet their physical needs.

Total mobilization

This evangelism should seek to mobilize the entire membership in witness. The objective is to have the whole church involved in some effective communication of the gospel.

Step Four—Learn to Take Care of Itself

The second of the three partial results to strive for as the young church matures is that it learn to *take care of itself* (see figure 62). Under normal circumstances, no one who does not take care of himself can be considered to be mature. In the plan I have presented, five distinct elements characterize a church that takes care of itself:

Meaningful worship

The ritual and ceremony of public worship must not be allowed to overshadow its essential meaning. Chapter 7 discussed much that is involved if worship is to be meaningful and efficacious. Since public worship is a necessity for God's people, extreme care must be shown in designing it.

Adequate administration

One of the main reasons for good management of the affairs and life of the local church is to facilitate the spiritual ministry of its members. Good administration, discussed in chapters 2 and 8, eliminates confusion and enables the Holy Spirit to accomplish his wonderful edifying ministry. I am convinced that the prevalence of "dictatorships" in many evangelical churches is a sign of a lack of adequate administration. Sometimes individuals become dictators by default—others are not functioning as they should. Some are willful dictators, incorrigible egotists. The New Testament records of the early churches do not reveal them as one-man shows. In church planting, *adequate* is a key word for describing administration. Only such administration as is absolutely necessary should be employed. Job descriptions are useful in conjunction with training and educational programs to equip those accepting positions of responsibility. A church constitution is basic to mutual understanding and discipline. Legal statutes and registration with the government should be secured by each local church as soon as possible. They will be necessary when acquiring property, if and when this is done.

Spiritual life

Here we are dealing with the very heart of the local church. If the kind of spiritual life described in chapter 6 is not present the congregation will be seriously deficient and even impotent. It will be incapable not only of caring for itself, but also of living for others. When speaking of the spiritual life of the church the following biblical truths must come into play. First, special attention must be given to the scriptural doctrine of stewardship, remembering that the financial is only one aspect of a much larger New Testament doctrine touching the very life of the believer. Stewardship teaching is a high priority in "making disciples." Second, it is not enough to teach believers that the Holy Spirit graciously gives every Christian the capacities for spiritual service. They must be encouraged and helped to fulfil these roles, serving one another in the power of the Spirit "as good stewards of the manifold grace of God" (1 Pet. 4:10). There is much talk *about* spiritual gifts, but little actual freedom in the churches to implement them. The local church is the loser, and the consequences for evangelism and church planting are tragic!

Third, those who teach and preach in the local church must become spiritually sensitive to congregational needs. This is what the New Testament is all about! Felt needs of the congregation should be satisfied. Sound, authoritative exhortation is lacking in the pulpit ministry much of the time. Christians in our churches must be challenged to be "doers of the word, and not merely hearers who delude themselves" (James 1:22). Fourth, a healthy human body serves as a New Testament model of how the local church should live. As members of one another with the Lord Jesus Christ as our Head, we should live in mutual harmony. God's love, manifested in the body, is demonstrated by caring, helpful fellowship. Such spiritual fruit is intimately related to the mutual exercise of the gifts of the Spirit. Fundamental to this doctrine concerning the local church as a body is the obvious, yet grossly neglected fact that every single believer is important (1 Cor. 12:14–25).

Financial stability

Christian missions ministering in countries with a weak economic base are tempted to "mercifully" provide financial aid in exaggerated amounts with little serious consideration of the practical consequences. Stewardship is closely related to financial stability. Giving should grow proportionately with growth in numbers. The church should live within its means and not be led to believe that living on other people's help is a healthy situation; it is not! Adults should live on their own earnings; they should not forever be dependent upon their parents and friends. If a new local church receives financial aid for one reason or another from the "mother" church or from any other outside source, it should be encouraged to free itself as soon as possible for its own good. Financially dependent churches do not plant new churches.

Conscious self-identity

The first believers—and later the new church congregation—need a healthy self-image. In the Christian body, each member needs to realize his personal worth to God, his personal responsibility to God, and his personal function as a living part of the body. Although evangelical churches around the world are small on the average and are few in number, they are of great worth in God's sight. They have a unique ministry to perform.

This fact can be greatly strengthened by a balanced biblical understanding of the church. Independence must be balanced by interdependence. It is healthy and encouraging to remember that the church of Jesus Christ is, after all, *one*. Its people are local members of the family of God (Eph. 1:22–23; 2:19–22, and 4:4–6). This family is, at every moment, world wide!

Step Five—Learn to Be Relevant to Its Cultural Surroundings

The effectiveness of evangelism in the vicinity of the church will depend to a great degree upon its relevancy. I recommended in chapter 11 that limited ethnographic investigation be pursued to better equip the churches and church planters for cultural contextualization. A workable, valid method for doing ethnography in the framework of church planting is a real necessity. Each culture includes characteristics to be commended and others to be condemned. Biblical theology is our measuring rod. The local church must know where to take its stand. Whether we see authentic, scriptural conversions from the world partly depends upon how clearly local people understand the message. Keys to achieving such an understanding are conceptualization, configuration, exposition, implications, and confrontation.

Through all of this runs a strategy that aims beyond planting churches throughout the world. We can and must plant churches that will plant churches that will plant churches that will plant churches until Jesus returns. Maranatha! Nothing less than this will begin to meet the tremendous need as we reach the year 2000 and beyond.

Appendix

The Feasibility Study: Subjects of Inquiry, page 184
Adapted from Ezra Earl Jones, *Strategies for New Churches* (New York: Harper & Row, 1976), 89–90.

Community Profile, pages 185–86
F. Jack Redford, *Planting New Churches* (Nashville: Broadman, 1978), Appendix A.

Area Analysis for Church Extension, pages 187–89
Redford, *Planting New Churches*, Appendix B.

Score Sheet for New Work Priority, page 190
Redford, *Planting New Churches*, Appendix C.

Overall Profile of Potential Target Community, pages 191–94
David J. Hesselgrave, *Planting Churches Cross-Culturally: A Guide for Home and Foreign Missions* (Grand Rapids: Baker, 1980), 101–4 (Fig. 10).

How to Plant a Church Capable of Reproducing Itself
Foldout chart designed by Samuel D. Faircloth, 1984. See inside-cover.

The Feasibility Study: Subjects of Inquiry

1. How many people live in the community now? What is the ultimate population of the community expected to be, and how rapid is the anticipated growth.

2. How mobile is the community?

3. Are the people moving in primarily: young families? middle aged couples? elderly? What lifestyles may be discerned? What is the racial character of the community? What is the income and educational level of the adults?

4. What types of housing are being constructed and in what proportion? Will the community be diverse or basically homogenous?

5. Have elementary schools been constructed, and where are they located?

6. What shopping areas have been provided for the community? Have they already been built or how soon may they be expected? Where will people shop if such facilities will not be available locally?

7. Where do the people who live in the area work? If it is primarily outside of the community, to what areas do they go?

8. Are all utilities now available or can they reasonably be expected to be added as needed?

9. Has a barrier, such as a major thoroughfare or limited-access highway, divided the community.

10. What is the availability of mortgage money and building materials? Is a time approaching when residential construction is likely to be halted, at least temporarily.

11. What is the reputation of this community through the rest of the city? Is it seen as a desirable or an undesirable place to live? Does its development have the support of political leaders? How have zoning and building laws been altered in a way that benefits this neighborhood?

12. Is there reason to believe that the religious character of the new residents differs from that of the area generally?

13. What other evangelical or mainline churches have been organized?

14. How close are other viable churches of the planting denomination to the proposed site of the new church? How will they be affected by the new church, based on present evidence? Are any of them now attracting new members from this community in significant numbers?

COMMUNITY PROFILE

DEPARTMENT OF CHURCH EXTENSION
HOME MISSION BOARD, SOUTHERN BAPTIST CONVENTION

Name of Area/Community:_____ State:_____

SECTION I - THE COMMUNITY:

1. Population: Now_____ 1970_____ 1960_____

2. Dimensions (approximate miles): North-South_____ East-West_____

3. Type of Housing (percent): Single Family___% Low-Rise Apartments___%

                         Town House___% High-Rise Apartments____%

4. Age of Housing: When was most of the housing built?_____
                                               Years

5. Type of Community: Inner City ☐   Established Neighborhood ☐

                  Suburban ☐ Exurban ☐ Small Town ☐ Open Country ☐

SECTION II - THE PEOPLE:

6. Age Characteristics (percent): Under 18 Years___% 18-39 Years_____%

                               40-64 Years_____% 65 Years or More____%

7. Race (percent): White_____% Negro_____% Other_____ _____%
                                                Name

8. Family Structure: Young Families With Children ☐ Young Couples ☐

                  Older Families Without Children ☐   Singles ☐

9. Employment: White Collar ☐   Blue Collar ☐   Military ☐

               University ☐   Other_____ ☐

10. Family Income Groups (percent): Less Than $4,000___% $4,000-$7,999___%

                               $8,000-$11,999___% $12,000-$15,999___%

                               $16,000-$19,000___% $20,000 or More___%

11. Nativity (percent): This State_____% This Region_____% Abroad_____%

12. Educational Attainment (percent): Grammar School___% High School_____%

                                     College_____%

Community Profile Continued

SECTION III - THE CHURCHES

13. On the chart below, please rank in descending order by size of total member-
    ship these denominations in the first column: Baptist, Catholic, Methodist,
    Presbyterian, Congregational, Christian, Episcopal, Lutheran, Pentacostal
    (all kinds), Jewish, and others. Then complete the information requested
    on each denomination.

LIST OF DENOMINATIONS	NUMBER		
	CHURCHES	MEMBERS	AVER. ATTEND.

Priority	Number
Association	State

AREA ANALYSIS FOR CHURCH EXTENSION

This analysis should be made before plans are finalized for the new church extension.

      (city)   (county)   (state)

Area's name (description of geographical area) _____

Association _____

1. RELIGIOUS DATA (Resource: personal interviews, telephone yellow pages, and observation):

   (1) How many denominations are presently represented in this area?

	Churches	Members
Southern Baptist		
Other Baptist		
Other evangelical		
Catholic		
Other nonevangelical		
Jewish		
Other religions		
TOTAL		

   (2) Rank the denominations represented in the area by name and membership:

Rank denominations by membership and write in names.	Number members	Number attendants	Number churches
1			
2			
3			
4			
5			

   (3) What percent of the people in the area attend religious services?

      Weekly_____ Monthly_____ Seldom_____ Never_____ = 100%

      Area Name _____

   (4) Does any Southern Baptist church attempt to reach this area now? _____

      How? _____

   (5) Name the nearest Southern Baptist church. _____

      a. How many miles is it from this area? _____

      b. What economic groups does it reach best?_____

(6) Name the Southern Baptist church(es) that is the logical one to sponsor this new work. _____

(7) How many unchurched persons are there in this area?

Unchurched persons	Number	Percent*
Baptist preference?		
Other preference?		
TOTAL		100%
Names and addresses in hand		
Have expressed an interest		

2. POPULATION DATA (Resource: 1970 Census and Planning Commission):

(1) What is the present population of the area by the racial and age groups listed below?

Racial Groups

Types	Number	Percent*
White		
Negro		
Spanish surname		
Other_____		
TOTAL		100%

Age Groups

By years	Number	Percent*
0-17 years		
18-34 years		
35-64 years		
65 and over		
TOTAL		100%

*Percent is calculated by dividing the total into the number in each group.

Area Name _____

(2) What are the present housing trends in this area?

Occupancy	Number	Percent*
Owner		
Renter		
TOTAL		100%

Type Housing	Units	Percent*
Single family		
Multifamily		
Mobile home		
TOTAL		100%

*Percent is calculated by dividing the total into the number in each group.

(3) Is this area's population (check more than one): Stable ☐   Growing ☐   New ☐

Declining ☐   Proposed ☐   Other ☐ _____

3. ECONOMIC DATA (Resource: Local office employment agency for State and Planning Commission)

(1) Describe the economy of the area. (agriculture, manufacturing, mining, government installations and insti-

tutions, military, commerce and trade, tourism, recreation, other) _____

(2) What are the five largest job classifications represented in the area? (agriculture, manufacturing, construc-

tion, transportation, trade, finance, service, mining and government) _____

(3) What percentage of the people are in each of the two following categories?

Employment Groups	Percent		Income Groups	Percent
Professional			Less than $3,000	
Office workers			$3,000 - $4,999	
Skilled			$5,000 $6,999	
Semiskilled			$7,000 - $9,999	
Unskilled			$10,000 - $14,999	
			$15,000 and over	
TOTAL	100%		TOTAL	100%

Area Name _____

4. INSTITUTIONAL DATA (school board, planning commission and observation):

(1) What educational institutions are present in the area?

Institution	Schools	Students
Primary		
Secondary		
Technical		
College and university		
TOTAL		

(2) Name any public institutions in the area. (mental or VA hospitals, prison, military, etc.) _____

_____

(3) Name any private institutions in the area. (retirement centers, rest homes, nursing homes, etc.) _____

_____

5. SUMMARY:

Use a separate sheet to write a summary of the area as you see it, and give your suggestions as to how this new work should begin (fellowship Bible class, VBS, branch Sunday School, chapel, revival, community ministries, week-day ministry, others).

This analysis was made by _____ Date_____

Position_____ of Association_____. State _____

Evaluated by _____. Evaluated by . _____
(associational superintendent of missions)   (state missions director)

If church pastoral aid is involved, make six copies of this survey — one each for: superintendent of missions; moderator; chairman of missions committee; sponsoring church; director of missions; Department of Church Extension, Home Mission Board, 1350 Spring Street, NW, Atlanta, Georgia 30309, (404) 873-4041.

NOTE — A copy of this survey must precede or accompany each application for church pastoral aid.

SCORE SHEET FOR NEW WORK PRIORITY

List communities and rate from 1-10.

See pages for priorities questions.	Buckhead	Palmetto	Sandy Springs	Decatur															
Population?	4	6	9	10															
Churched?	3	4	7	7															
Response?	3	3	5	6															
Potential?	4	5	7	9															
Strategic?	3	4	7	7															
Influence?	4	5	6	8															
Self-Support?	4	5	8	8															
Resources?	3	5	8	8															
Sponsorship?	4	5	7	9															
Field?	3	4	6	8															
Nucleus?	4	5	7	7															
Personnel?	3	4	5	7															
Alternative?	4	5	6	8															
Total?	46	60	87	103															
Score Number	4	3	2	1															
Rating	L	M	H	VH															

1. Select communities from compilation.
2. Rate 1-10.   1-lowest rating;   10-highest rating.
   Rating is relative and communities must be compared to each other in each area.
3. Score: highest #1, next highest #2, etc.
4. Rating is a relative guide to help determine priorities:
   20-50 low, 50-75 medium, 75-100 high, 100-130 very high

Overall Profile
of
Potential Target Community

I. Map

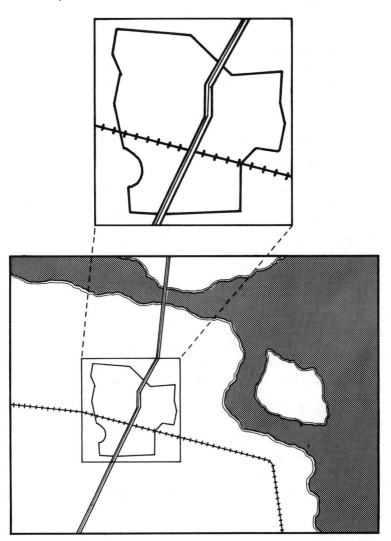

II. Geographical Profile

    Section A—Description of the Land

      1. Rolling Hills_____%   4. Mountains _____%

      2. Plains _____%   5. Forests _____%

      3. Rivers &
         Streams _____%

    Section B—Land Use

      1. Farming _____%   4. Commercial_____%

      2. Ranching _____%   5. Unused _____%

      3. Lumber _____%   6. Other _____%

    Section C—Transportation

      1. Railroads

      2. Roads

      3. Airport

      4. Rivers

Analysis: _____

_____

III. Population Profile

    Section A—Population

      1. Population in 1970 _____, 1980 _____, 1990 _____

      2. Present population _____

      3. Density (number of persons per square mile) _____

    Section B—Population Growth or Decline

      1. Population growth or decline 1970–1990:

        a. Growth _____ (_____%)

        b. Decline _____ (_____%)

      2. Population projections for 1995 _____ 2000 _____
        2010 _____

Analysis: _____

_____

IV. Economic Profile

Section A—Occupation

1. Farming or ranching   ——%
2. Business and clerical   ——%
3. Education   ——%
4. Government or military——%
5. Other——   ——%

Section B—Income

1. Less than   X   ——%
2. Between   X and Y   ——%
3. More than   Y   ——%

Analysis: _____

_____

V. Sociological Profile

Table A—Ethnic Groupings

1. _____ (%)
2. _____ (%)
3. _____ (%)
Etc.

Table B—Classes, Castes, Clans

1. _____ (%)
2. _____ (%)
3. _____ (%)
Etc.

Table C—Age

1. Under 18 _____ (%)
2. Between 19 and 35 _____ (%)
3. Between 36 and 50 _____ (%)
4. Over 51 _____ (%)

Analysis: _____

_____

VI. Religious Profile

Table A—Christian Population

1. Roman Catholic _____%   4. Conservative
2. Eastern Orthodox _____%   Protestant _____%
3. Liberal Protestant _____%   5. Other _____%

Table B—Non-Christian

1. Muslim _____%   4. Jewish _____%
2. Hindu _____%   5. Unaffiliated _____%
3. Buddhist _____%   6. Other _____%

Analysis: _____

_____

VII. Overall Evaluation

_____

_____

_____

_____

Bibliography

Allen, Louis A. *The Management Profession*. New York: McGraw-Hill, 1964.

Allen, Roland. *The Spontaneous Expansion of the Church and the Causes Which Hinder It*. Grand Rapids: Eerdmans, 1962.

Armerding, Hudson T. *Leadership*. Wheaton: Tyndale, 1978.

Banks, Robert. *Paul's Idea of Community*. Grand Rapids: Eerdmans, 1988.

Barrett, David B., ed. *World Christian Encyclopedia*. New York, Oxford University Press, 1982.

Barrett, Lois. *Building the House Church*. Scottdale, Pa.: Herald, 1986.

Benjamin, Paul. *The Growing Congregation*. Lincoln, Ill.: Lincoln Christian College Press, 1972.

Beyerhaus, Peter. *Shaken Foundations: Theological Foundations for Mission*. Grand Rapids: Zondervan, 1972.

Beyerhaus, Peter, and Henry Lefever. *The Responsible Church and the Foreign Mission*. Grand Rapids: Eerdmans, 1964.

Birkey, Del. *The House Church*. Scottdale, Pa.: Herald, 1988.

Boer, Harry R. *Pentecost and Missions*. Grand Rapids: Eerdmans, 1961.

Brock, Charles. *The Principles and Practice of Indigenous Church Planting*. Nashville: Broadman, 1981.

Brown, Arthur S. *How One Church Can Start Another*. Chicago: Conservative Baptist Foreign Mission Society, 1957.

Bruce, Alexander Balmain. *The Training of the Twelve*. New Canaan, Conn.: Keats, 1979.

Burton, Ernest De Witt. *A Critical and Exegetical Commentary on the Epistle to the Galatians*. New York: C. Scribner's Sons, 1920.

Chafer, Lewis Sperry. *He That Is Spiritual*. Grand Rapids: Dunham, 1965; repr. ed., Grand Rapids: Zondervan, 1974.

195

Chaney, Charles L., and Ron S. Lewis. *Design for Church Growth*. Nashville: Broadman, 1977.

Coleman, Robert E. *The Master Plan of Evangelism*. Westwood, N.J.: Revell, 1963.

Collins, Gary. *How to Be a People Helper*. Santa Ana, Calif.: Vision House, 1976.

Conant, Judson E. *Every-Member Evangelism*. New York: Harper and Brothers, 1922.

Conn, Harvie M. *Evangelism: Doing Justice and Preaching Grace*. Grand Rapids: Zondervan, 1982.

Cook, Richard B. "Paul, the Organizer." *Missiology* 9 (October 1981): 485–98.

Cosgrove, Francis M., Jr. *Essentials of New Life*. Colorado Springs, Colo.: Navpress, 1980.

Costas, Orlando E. *The Church and Its Mission: A Shattering Critique from the Third World*. Wheaton: Tyndale House, 1974.

_____. *The Integrity of Mission: The Inner Life and Outreach of the Church*. New York: Harper and Row, 1979.

Dayton, Edward R. *God's Purpose/Man's Plans—A Workbook*. Monrovia, Calif.: Missions Advanced Research and Communications Center, 1978.

Dayton, Edward R., and Ted W. Engstrom. *Strategy for Leadership*. Old Tappan, N.J.: Revell, 1979.

Dayton, Edward R., and David A. Fraser. *Planning Strategies for World Evangelization*. Grand Rapids: Eerdmans, 1980.

Detzler, Wayne A. *The Changing Church in Europe: Religious Movements Since 1960*. Grand Rapids: Zondervan, 1978.

Douglas, J. D., ed. *Let the Earth Hear His Voice*. Minneapolis: World Wide, 1975.

_____, ed. *The New Bible Dictionary*. London: Inter-Varsity Fellowship, 1962.

Drummond, Lewis A. *Leading Your Church in Evangelism*. Nashville: Broadman, 1975.

Edwards, Gene. *How to Have a Soul Winning Church*. Tyler, Tex.: Soul Winning, 1962.

Eims, LeRoy. *Be the Leader You Were Meant to Be: What the Bible Says About Leadership*. Wheaton: Victor, 1975.

Engel, James F. *How Can I Get Them to Listen?* Grand Rapids: Zondervan, 1977.

_____. *How to Communicate the Gospel Effectively*. Ghana, West Africa: Africa Christian, 1988.

Engel, James F., and H. Wilbert Norton. *What's Gone Wrong with the Harvest?* Grand Rapids: Zondervan, 1975.

Fleming, Bruce C. E. *Contextualization of Theology: An Evangelical Assessment*. Pasadena, Calif.: William Carey Library, 1980.

Flynn, Leslie B. *Nineteen Gifts of the Spirit: Which Do You Have?* Wheaton: Victor, 1974.

Gangel, Kenneth O. *Competent to Lead*. Chicago: Moody, 1974.

Gerber, Vergil, ed. *Discipling Through Theological Education by Extension: A Fresh Approach to Theological Education in the 1980s*. Chicago: Moody, 1980.

_____. *God's Way to Keep a Church Going and Growing*. Glendale, Calif.: Regal, 1974.

Getz, Gene A. *Sharpening the Focus of the Church*. Chicago: Moody, 1974.

_____. *A Biblical Theology of Material Possessions*. Chicago: Moody, 1990.

_____. *The Measure of a Church*. Glendale, Calif.: Regal, 1975.

Glasser, Arthur F., and Donald A. McGavran. *Contemporary Theologies of Mission*. Grand Rapids: Baker, 1983.

Green, Michael. *Evangelism in the Early Church*. London: Hodder and Stoughton, 1970.

Greenway, Roger S. *Apostles to the City: Biblical Strategies for Urban Missions*. Grand Rapids: Baker, 1978.

Gross, Edward N. *Is Charles Kraft an Evangelical?* Collingswood, N.J.: Christian Beacon, 1985.

Hansen, B. J. *Practical PERT*. Washington, D.C.: America House, 1964.

Hay, Alexander R. *New Testament Order for Church and Missionary*. Audubon, N.J.: New Testament Missionary Union, 1947.

Hendrix, Olan. *Management and the Christian Worker*. Manila, Philippines: Living Books for All, 1972.

Henrichsen, Walter A. *Disciples Are Made—Not Born*. Wheaton: Victor, 1974.

Hesselgrave, David J. *Communicating Christ Cross-Culturally: An Introduction to Missionary Communication*. Grand Rapids: Zondervan , 1978.

_____. *Dynamic Christian Movements*. Grand Rapids: Baker, 1978.

_____. *Planting Churches Cross-Culturally: A Guide for Home and Foreign Missions*. Grand Rapids: Baker, 1980.

_____, ed. *Theology and Mission: Papers Given at Trinity Consultation No. 1*. Grand Rapids: Baker, 1978.

Hesselgrave, David J., and Edward Rommen. *Contextualization: Meanings, Methods, and Models*. Grand Rapids: Baker, 1989.

Hodges, Melvin L. *A Guide to Church Planting*. Chicago: Moody, 1973.

Jones, Ezra Earl. *Strategies for New Churches*. New York: Harper & Row, 1976.

Joslin, Roy. *Urban Harvest*. Hertfordshire, England: Evangelical, 1982.

Kendall, R. T. *Tithing*. London: Hodder and Stoughton, 1982.

Keyes, Lawrence E. *The Last Age of Missions*. Pasadena, Calif.: William Carey Library, 1983.

Kilinski, Kenneth K., and Jerry C. Wofford. *Organization and Leadership in the Local Church*. Grand Rapids: Zondervan, 1973.

Kraft, Charles H. *Christianity in Culture: A Study in Dynamic Biblical Theologizing in Cross-Cultural Perspective*. Maryknoll, N.Y.: Orbis, 1979.

Krupp, Nate. *You Can Be a Soul Winner—Here's How*. Wheaton: Lay Evangelism, 1963.

Kunz, Marilyn, and Catherine Schell. *How to Start a Neighborhood Bible Study*. New York: Neighborhood Bible Studies, 1966.

————. *Mark: Seventeen Discussions for Group Bible Study*. Dobbs Ferry, N.Y.: Neighborhood Bible Studies, 1963.

Lausanne Occasional Papers. *No. 9: Thailand Report—Christian Witness to Large Cities*. Wheaton:˙Lausanne Committee for World Evangelization, 1980.

————. *No. 10: Thailand Report—Christian Witness to Nominal Christians among Roman Catholics*. Wheaton: Lausanne Committee for World Evangelization, 1980.

————. *No. 12: Thailand Report—Christian Witness to Marxists*. Wheaton: Lausanne Committee for World Evangelization, 1980.

————. *No. 20: An Evangelical Commitment to Simple Life-Style: Exposition and Commentary*. Wheaton: Lausanne Committee for World Evangelization, 1980.

————. *No. 21: Grand Rapids Report—Evangelism and Social Responsibility: An Evangelical Commitment*. Wheaton: Lausanne Committee for World Evangelization, 1982.

Lindholm, Paul R. *Principles and Practice of Christian Stewardship*. Madras, India: Christian Literature Society, 1965.

Lingenfelter, Sherwood G., and Marvin K. Mayers. *Ministering Cross-Culturally*. Grand Rapids: Baker, 1986.

Lukasse, Johan. *Churches with Roots: Planting Churches in Post-Christian Europe*. Bromiley, Kent, England: STL, 1990

Luzbetak, Louis J. *The Church and Cultures: An Applied Anthropology for the Religious Worker*. Techny, Ill.: Divine Word, 1970.

McGavran, Donald A. "Try These Seven Steps for Planting Churches," *Global Church Growth Bulletin* 18 (May–June 1981): 110–13, 116.

————. *Understanding Church Growth*. Grand Rapids: Eerdmans, 1970; rev. ed., Grand Rapids: Eerdmans, 1980.

Meeks, Wayne A. *The First Urban Christians: The Social World of the Apostle Paul*. New Haven, Conn.: Yale University Press, 1982.

Miller, C. John. *Outgrowing the Ingrown Church*. Grand Rapids: Zondervan, 1986.

Miller, Keith. *The Taste of New Wine*. Waco, Tex.: Word, 1965.

Monsma, Timothy. *An Urban Strategy for Africa*. Pasadena, Calif.: William Carey Library, 1979.

Morrisey, George L. *Management by Objectives and Results in the Public Sector*. Reading, Mass.: Addison-Wesley, 1976.

Murphy, Edward F. *Spiritual Gifts and the Great Commission*. South Pasadena, Calif.: Mandate, 1975.

Neighbour, Ralph W., Jr. *Baptist Strategy Report: Brussels*. Brussels, Belgium: Belgian Baptist Mission, 1983.

————. *Brisbane: Resistant or Neglected?* Ferny Hills, Queensland: Touch International Ministries, 1987.

_____. *Knocking on Doors, Opening Hearts,* 2d ed. Houston: Touch Outreach Ministries, 1990.

_____. *Spiritual Gifts Inventory.* Houston: Touch Outreach Ministries, 1985.

_____. *The Shepherd's Guidebook.* Houston: Touch Outreach Ministries, 1988.

_____. *Urban Evangelization Strategy: Basic Training Manual.* Singapore: Singapore Baptist Convention, 1977.

_____. *The Way Home.* Houston: Touch Outreach Ministries; Colorado Springs: International Bible Society, 1986.

_____. *Where Do We Go From Here? A Guidebook for the Cell Group Church.* Houston: Touch Outreach Ministries, 1990.

Nevius, John. *Planting and Development of Missionary Churches,* 4th ed. Philadelphia: Presbyterian and Reformed, 1958.

Nida, Eugene A., and William D. Reyburn. *Meaning across Cultures.* Maryknoll, N.Y.: Orbis, 1981.

Olford, Stephen F. *Heart Cry for Revival.* London: Marshall, Morgan and Scott, Ltd., 1963.

Pate, Larry. *Starting New Churches.* Brussels, Belgium: International Correspondence Institute, 1984.

Patterson, George A. *Applying Biblical Extension Principles.* La Ceiba, Honduras: Extension Bible Institute, n.d.

_____. *Church Planting Through Obedience Oriented Teaching.* Pasadena, Calif.: William Carey Library, 1981.

_____. *Congregation Progress Chart.* La Ceiba, Honduras: Extension Bible Institute, n.d.

_____. *Obedience Oriented Education.* Portland, Ore.: n.p., 1976.

Pentecost, J. Dwight. *Design for Discipleship.* Grand Rapids: Zondervan, 1971.

Schaller, Lyle E. *Looking in the Mirror.* Nashville: Abingdon, 1984.

Schmidt, Karl Ludwig. " Ἐκκλησία." Gerhard Kittel, ed. *Theological Dictionary of the New Testament,* vol. 3. Grand Rapids: Eerdmans, 1965.

Shelley, Bruce L. *What Baptists Believe.* Wheaton: Conservative Baptist, 1973.

Shenk, David W., and Ervin R. Stutzman. *Creating Communities of the Kingdom.* Scottdale, Pa.: Herald, 1988.

Snyder, Howard A. *The Problem of Wine Skins: Church Structure in a Technological Age.* Downers Grove, Ill.: Inter-Varsity, 1975.

Soltau, Theodore Stanley. *Missions at the Crossroads.* Wheaton: Van Kampen, 1954.

Spradley, James P. *Participant Observation.* New York: Holt, Rinehart and Winston, 1980.

_____. *The Ethnographic Interview.* New York: Holt, Rinehart and Winston, 1979.

Stedman, Ray C. *Body Life,* 2d ed. Glendale, Calif.: Regal, 1972.

Stephens, Ken. *Discipleship Evangelism.* Scottsdale, Ariz.: Good Life, 1978.

Stott, John R. W. *Christian Mission in the Modern World*. Downers Grove, Ill.: Inter-Varsity, 1975.

_____. *The Baptism and Fullness of the Holy Spirit*. Downers Grove, Ill.: Inter-Varsity, 1974; 2d ed., *Baptism and Fullness: The Work of the Holy Spirit Today*. Downers Grove, Ill.: Inter-Varsity, 1976.

Tippett, Allan R. *Introduction to Missiology*. Pasadena, Calif.: William Carey Library, 1987.

Unger, Merrill F. *The Baptism and Gifts of the Holy Spirit*. Chicago: Moody, 1974.

Verkuyl, Johannes. *Contemporary Missiology: An Introduction*. Translated by Dale Cooper. Grand Rapids: Eerdmans, 1978.

Wagner, C. Peter. *Church Growth and the Whole Gospel: A Biblical Mandate*. San Francisco: Harper & Row, 1981.

_____. *Frontiers in Missionary Strategy*. Chicago: Moody, 1971.

Warren, Richard, and William A. Shell. *Twelve Dynamic Bible Study Methods*. Wheaton: Victor, 1983.

Waterman, Leonard P. *A Manual for Starting New Churches*. Wheaton: Conservative Baptist, 1979.

Watts, Wayne. *The Gift of Giving*. Colorado Springs, Colo.: Navpress, 1982.

Index